GENERAL LIBRARY
DISTRICT GENERAL HOSPITAL
MOORGATE
ROTHERHAM

WITHDRAWN FROM
ROTHERHAM PUBLIC
LIBRARIES
DGH GL

- 9 OCT 1992   24 SEP 1998

2 1 JUL 1993   30 MAR 2001

17 DEC 1993   - 2 NOV 2002
- 2 AUG 1995   2 NOV 2002
                      A 4.
2 5 AUG 1995   19 JUL 2003

Derm
25 JAN 1996   - 7 APR 2004

1 0 JUN 1996

2 8 JUN 1996

1 1 SEP 1996

18 SEP 1996

2 0 JUN 1997

AUTOMOBILE
ASSOCIATION

Yorkshire Dales
2nd Ed

43218

£9.38Net MBC

460 4612
1348 536 492

ROTHERHAM PUBLIC LIBRARIES

This book must be returned by the date specified at the time of
issue as the Date Due for Return.
The loan may be extended (personally, by post or telephone) for
a further period, if the book is not required by another reader,
by quoting the above number
LM1 (C)

ORDNANCE SURVEY LEISURE GUIDE

YORKSHIRE DALES

▲ River Swale near Marske

Produced jointly by the Publishing Division of
The Automobile Association and the Ordnance Survey

Editorial contributors: Laurie Fallows (A Day in the Life of a Dalesman, Recreation in the Dales, Walks); Rebecca Snelling (Fact File); Colin Speakman (The Pennine Way through the Dales, Tours, Walks); Dr A C Waltham (Limestone Scenery); Geoffrey N Wright (The Story of the Dales, A to Z Gazetteer and Gazetteer revisions for new edition).

Original photography: Oliver Mathews and John Morrison

Typeset by Avonset, Midsomer Norton, Bath
Colour separation by BTB Colour Reproduction Ltd., Whitchurch, Hampshire
Printed and bound by William Clowes Limited, Beccles and London

Maps extracted from the Ordnance Survey's 1:50 000 Landranger Series and reduced to a scale of 1:63 360, 1:25 000 Outdoor Leisure Series, and 1:250 000 Routemaster Series with the permission of Her Majesty's Stationery Office. Crown copyright.

Additions to the maps by the Cartographic Department of The Automobile Association and the Ordnance Survey.

Produced by the Publishing Division of The Automobile Association.

Distributed in the United Kingdom by the Ordnance Survey, Southampton, and the Publishing Division of The Automobile Association, Fanum House, Basingstoke, Hampshire RG21 2EA.

First edition 1985
Reprinted 1987, 1988, 1989
Revised edition 1992

A CIP catalogue record of this book is available from the British Library.

AA ISBN 0 7495 0388 2 (hardback)
AA ISBN 0 7495 0378 5 (softback)
OS ISBN 0 319 00287 X (hardback)
OS ISBN 0 319 00278 0 (softback)

Published by The Automobile Association and the Ordnance Survey.

Introduction: Angram from Kisdon Hill, Swaledale

Contents

▲ Hawes, Wensleydale

Introduction

Limestone escarpments, drystone walls, sweeping fells and rushing becks, crags and scars gleaming in the sunlight are all part of the unique Dales landscape described within these pages. Whether you are in search of solitude or the bustle of the busy market towns, this guide will provide the key. It explores the history, traditions and geology and describes the towns, villages and hamlets of the Dales. Walks and motor tours seek out the hidden corners and the finest scenery. Written entirely by people who live and work in the Yorkshire Dales, backed by the AA's research expertise and the Ordnance Survey's mapping, this is equally useful to the faithful who return to the Dales year after year and to the first-time visitor.

The Story of the Dales

J B Priestley once said, 'In all my travels I've never seen a countryside to equal in beauty the Yorkshire Dales. The Dales have never disappointed me.' A more recent writer, James Herriot, describes the occasion when he first realised the magic of the Dales, as he was driving along the unfenced moorland road between Leyburn and Grinton, and stopped to look down into Swaledale. 'I was captivated, completely spellbound and I still am to this day.' What, then, is there about the Yorkshire Dales which casts its spell upon so many who visit the area, what quality makes the Dales unique?

Healaugh's grassed terraces were ploughed by the early Anglian farmers who settled in Swaledale from the 7th century

More than anything else it is a blend of the right ingredients of landscape mixed in the right proportions, painted in the right colours whatever the season, and humanised by the handwork of man over fifty generations. From the eastern margins of the Dales along the edge of the Vale of York the land gradually rises westwards. Moors sweep steadily upwards as long, broad ridges to the high fells of the Pennines where a score of summits reach to over 2000 feet. On their lonely uplands are some of the last primeval wilderness areas of England, with spacious solitude, yet never loneliness. Fresh winds sough and moan through tussocky grass and springy heather, to buffet against dark crags of gritstone or crisp limestone scars. There is nothing quite so penetrating as lashing Pennine rain; there are days of quiet calm, though never of silence, for the sounds of the hills are always present. Nothing is so evocative as the bubbling, liquid mystery of curlew-call, the harsh rasp of grouse, lapwing lament, piping of golden plover, skylark-song or sheep-voices borne along the breeze.

Water is one of the ingredients common to the uplands and the valleys. On the high fells spongy peat and squelching green moss help to generate the moorland becks which tumble and frolic down the fellsides, mingle and meet, and leap over waterfalls into small dark pools, create their own charming gills, and finally join the main rivers. Dozens of separate little dales contribute their individual themes into the whole great symphony of the Dales.

Swaledale is narrow, sinuous, grand and touched with the melancholy of former industry. Wensleydale is broad, green, generously wooded, given added distinction by two noble castles. Wharfedale is sylvan, always lovely, with a benediction bestowed by Bolton Priory. Malhamdale and Ribblesdale embrace the Craven crescent, where the limestone bones of landscape are near the surface, creating cliffs, crags and scars white-gleaming in sunlight, yet having contrasting, cavernous depths beneath the ground. A team of lesser dales, not always traversed by through roads, plays supporting roles – Arkengarthdale, Bishopdale, Colsterdale, Cotterdale, Coverdale, Crummackdale, Dentdale, Garsdale, Grisdale, Littondale and Walden.

Visual harmony
Throughout the Dales there is visual harmony both in the intimate scene or in the wide view from a windy hill. Colour is abundant but always soft and muted, greens and greys and many shades of brown; delicate tints of late-arriving spring, darkening maturity of summer meadows, purple of August heather, russet and silver of bracken and birch after the swallows and swifts have fled southwards. Brightest colours come from sky-reflecting waters of rivers, lakes and lonely tarns, or the scattered accents of wild flowers on limestone pastures and scars.

Stone walls impose their patterned geometry across valley floors or arrow up the sides of fells, white limestone in Craven country, dark sandstone elsewhere. Textures display variety and contrasts – gritstone beneath the hands, soft springiness of sheep's wool, cool water through fingers, and the friendly feel of sheltering walls. Natural scents and smells add their own joys: hay in field and barn, wild thyme on grassy swards, heather in bloom, new-dipped sheep, fungi in autumn woods, wood-smoke.

Man's effect on the landscape
The Yorkshire Dales is a farming landscape. Ice and eroding elements smoothed hillsides and valleys but man has changed the landscape most of all. Revealed in names of its natural features, its villages and hamlets, are twelve centuries of settlement and occupation, now dignified by stone cottages, farms and small houses of Georgian times, scattered along a street, facing across a green, or clustered together in a close community. Strong castles and ruined abbeys recall contrasts of medieval power; churches are long, low and broad, usually more humble than ostentatious. In moorland valleys remote from roads the remains of old workings evoke memories of men's struggle for lead-ore, coal and stone. Green lanes where monks trod, packhorses plodded and stock was driven are now used by walkers and others who find contentment or challenge in high and quiet places.

The rhythm of the seasons

With its soft green turf, limestone scars etching hillsides, the insistent presence of stone walls, stone field barns, and stone farms, this could be nowhere else in England. Only the Yorkshire Dales possess the magic proportions of shapes, lines, colours, textures, sounds, voices and people. Local folk cling to their heritage of the hills, and life in the Dales keeps to the natural rhythm of the seasons – lambing in April, clipping in early July, hay-timing later in the month, tupping in November, foddering during the winter months, and throughout the year the twice-daily demands of milking. Upon this seasonal pattern of life are superimposed the weekly market and the annual show. The changelessness of the pastoral cycle against a background of friendly hills is a satisfying anchorage in a troubled world. People find a warm reassurance in the Yorkshire Dales.

'Dale' is a Norse word for valley, so the area is well-named. Rivers of the main valleys – Swale, Ure, Nidd, Wharfe and Aire flow eastwards or south-eastwards to the Vale of York and the meandering Ouse. A few rivers take the shorter, steeper westwards course from the Pennine watershed, the Rawthey, Clough and Dee joining the Lune near Sedbergh, while the contrary Ribble, flowing southwards, eventually forsakes Yorkshire for Lancashire. Dozens of smaller dales fill out the family group, each an individual, but each with a family likeness. The whole area enjoys a unity given by the common platform of carboniferous rocks, with the Howgills of the north-west imparting a slatey counterpoint. Limestone of the Craven country in the south of the Dales dips gently to the east and north, there to be overlaid by the Yoredale Series of rocks – alternating layers of shale, sandstone and limestone, subsequently topped by Millstone Grit, whose remnants make flat summits to the higher fells, and whose dark moorlands are the wettest and most desolate areas of the Dales.

The Strid becomes a foaming torrent on its rapid course through Wharfedale

It is the strata sequences of the Yoredale Series which are largely responsible for the characteristic scenery of Wharfedale and Wensleydale. The limestones weather as long horizontal scars, while the softer shales above them are easily eroded into flat surfaces. The sandstones, usually hidden beneath the scree debris of the next limestone layer, have provided the good stones for the walls and roofs of most Dales buildings. Above the Yoredales but below the Millstone Grit are thin seams of coal, some of which, particularly around the head of Arkengarthdale and Swaledale, above Bishopdale, Coverdale, Dentdale and Garsdale, have been worked for centuries, the last pit near Tan Hill eventually ceasing in the mid-1930s.

The Ice Age

During the Ice Age that ended about 10,000 BC, snow and ice covered most of the northern hills, only the summits above about 2100 feet remaining ice-free. Glaciers flowed outwards from the high land, along existing valleys, scouring the landscapes, smoothing hillsides, and carrying debris and soil, subsequently spread as boulder-clay on valley-floors – more thickly at their lower ends. Moraines which formed during the retreat of glaciers have provided gravelly sites later chosen as well-drained areas for settlement. The Ice Age also affected soils, formed from the underlying rocks. Limestone soils are well-drained, light, rich in calcium, and yield good pasture with a large variety of plants. Millstone Grit uplands have acid, sandy and peaty soils, with fewer plant species. In Wharfedale and Wensleydale the different rock strata have resulted in a variety of soils, and along the valley sides vegetation tends to be zoned in relation to the strata.

After the Ice Age, with the climate becoming

This Roman road leads over the moors to the fort at Bainbridge

milder and damper, vegetation established itself; in 5000 BC the tree-line was about 1700 feet (as it is now), with birch, hazel, pine, oak, elm, alder and willow clothing the hillsides. By 3000 BC some New Stone Age settlement appears to have existed on lower slopes, and 'henge' sites at Castle Dykes above Aysgarth, and at Yarnbury above Grassington, are evidence of Bronze Age usage about 2000 BC. Small Middle Bronze Age stone circles can be seen at Carperby in Wensleydale, and Appletreewick, Bordley, Embsay and Yockenthwaite in the Wharfedale area. By 100 BC Celts reached the Dales area, mingled with the existing native Brigantine tribes, and established an Iron Age culture, favouring for their pastoral farming the well-drained, limestone soils of the Craven uplands. On Ingleborough's exposed summit plateau is the only Iron Age hill-fort in the Dales, extending over 15 acres and enclosed by a wall 3000 feet long.

The Roman invasion
The Roman occupation of Britain left few marks in the Dales. The most prominent site is the fort of Virosidum on a natural low hill to the east of Bainbridge in Wensleydale, garrisoned almost continuously from 80 AD to about 400 AD. This was linked to the major fort at Lancaster by a road whose course today can be followed, mainly on foot, running south-west from Bainbridge, crossing the fells as a walled lane before descending to the Ribble valley above Gearstones, where it joins the B6255 to Chapel-le-Dale and then follows a minor road to Ingleton. Another Roman road crosses from Bainbridge, by way of Stalling Busk and the Stake, to Cray and Buckden in Wharfedale. The rest of its course to the fort of Olicana (Ilkley) has not been definitely identified.

Today's pattern of settlement was largely established through successive waves of colonisation by Angles, Danes and Norsemen between the 7th and 11th centuries. Early settlement was from the east – placename elements '-ley', '-ham', and '-ton', are pointers to this. Danish colonisers following later tended to in-fill between Anglian villages, with '-by' and '-thorpe' representing their chosen sites. In the 10th century Norse families, moving across the Pennines from their footholds in Cumbria and on the Irish seaboard, infiltrated the upper dales, coming into Arkengarthdale, upper Swaledale above Gunnerside, Wensleydale above Askrigg, Wharfedale above Buckden, as well as the western valleys.

The Norse settlers
Whereas Anglian and Danish settlers kept stock, cultivated the land and tended to live in communities, the Norse settlers brought with them a tradition of pastoral farming, grazing the valley pastures in spring and autumn, moving to higher land during summer months. Their summer shielings were called 'saetrs', an element which appears in the names of hamlets in upper Wensleydale – Appersett, Burtersett, Countersett and Marsett.

Landscape features were important to these Norse farmers who spent so much of their lives on the uplands, and from whom we have derived those evocative names – beck, clint, crag, fell, gill, mere, moss, rigg, scar and tarn – words whose euphony is characteristic both of the western Yorkshire dales and hills and of those of Lakeland. It seems probable that the village greens which we appreciate today at Arncliffe, East Witton, Linton, Redmire, Reeth and West Burton may have originated as central areas in Anglian villages where the community could safely corral its livestock, should danger threaten. A certain amount of Norse influence survives today in the dialect of the Dalesman.

An 18th-century engraving of Bolton Castle

The Norman lords

Norman influence on the Dales landscape was limited. The great Domesday survey stopped at the edge of forest land – Reeth, Askrigg, Starbotton and Stainforth were forest-edge villages. In the later years of the 12th century the next settlements up the valleys were built as foresters' villages – Healaugh in Swaledale, Bainbridge in Wensleydale, Buckden in Wharfedale. The new Norman aristocracy set aside forest land for hunting, applying an early form of conservation, protecting deer, wild boar and otter for this specific purpose. From their great castles at Richmond and Middleham the Norman lords hunted Arkengarthdale Forest, Wensleydale Forest and Bishopdale Chase, while Langstrothdale Chase – still the name given to upper Wharfedale – was the preserve of the de Romilles and Cliffords of Skipton Castle.

Monastic landowners

A more peaceful, and from the point of view of land-use, a more profound, influence on the Dales landscape was that extending over four centuries by the monasteries. In 1132 Cistercian monks founded Fountains Abbey near Ripon, and twelve years later, Jervaulx Abbey in lower Wensleydale. Augustinian canons settled at Bolton Priory in Wharfedale in 1155, and smaller foundations were established at Coverham, Easby, Ellerton and Marrick. These, together with monasteries beyond the Dales area, owned huge areas of uplands throughout the Dales. The new monastic landowners brought great farming and sheep-breeding skills; they successfully managed their vast estates, running a pastoral economy through a series of granges, each responsible to the mother-house, but worked by lay-brothers and local labour. To a large extent they laid the foundations not only of the hill-farming scene of today but much of the present network of roads and tracks. In addition they drained marshy land, cleared scrubland, and built some of the earliest walls in the Dales; monastic records reveal that during the 13th century it was increasingly a common practice on estates to enclose small fields by stone walls, primarily to exclude other animals.

By the end of the 15th century feudal power had declined, although Middleham Castle was still in royal hands, Bolton Castle belonged to the Scropes, and Skipton Castle to the Cliffords. Threats from beyond the Scottish Border were still sufficiently real to merit the building of fortified houses – Nappa Hall in Wensleydale, Walburn Hall near Leyburn, and Barden Tower

Fountains Abbey, near Ripon

in Wharfedale, all of 15th-century date. The Dissolution of the Monasteries, 1537–40, saw the end of monastic ownership in the Dales; abbeys and priories became local quarries for good building stone, but it was not until about 1600 that the period of farmhouse building really started in the Dales. Although a few farmhouses and yeomen's houses date from the decades before the Civil War the greatest wave of rebuilding occurred between 1670 and 1700, with a second phase from 1720–50, this one coinciding with a Georgian improvement to existing houses.

Local stone – preferably sandstone – was used exclusively. Some buildings, especially in the lower Dales and around Bolton Abbey in Wharfedale, have been found still to retain their cruck-framed timbers, hidden behind stone exteriors. But throughout the Dales the unity of building-stones and styles has produced a rare harmony between buildings and their environment. Farmhouses, traditional barns, smaller houses and cottages look right in the landscape; they have, indeed, grown from it.

Generally speaking buildings are functional rather than fanciful; local prosperity was never great enough to merit unnecessary ostentation. The traditional 17th-century house showed a long, rectangular plan, two or three bays wide, but only one room deep, with a front entrance and sometimes an attached barn or shippon emphasising the horizontal lines. Offshuts at the rear were often later additions. From about 1720 the Georgian style infiltrated the Dales, possibly through the influence of Fountain Hospital at Linton; houses were higher, squarer, with a central doorway, vertical sash windows, and using good masonry mouldings. This style persisted, with modifications, until Victorian times, by when large numbers of small, humble cottages had been added to the village scene to house the lead-miners, quarrymen, millworkers and artisans who laboured in small local industries. But local stone continued to be used, and the low pitch (30 degrees) of stone-slate roofs still echoed the slopes of background hills.

Above: Haytiming in Littondale
Left: Farming methods in the 1940s

Land management

Between about 1760 and 1840, with a concentration of 20 years each side of 1800, most valley land and the lower hillsides were enclosed by stone walls, hundreds of miles of them. This was done mainly to manage the land more efficiently, control stock-breeding, and improve crop-yields. Barns were built or rebuilt. Shelter-belts and small woodlands were planted. New roads and lanes were aligned between newly-enclosed fields. Thus, today's landscape pattern is largely one of late 18th- and early 19th-century creation – a thousand years later than the settlement pattern. The two illustrate the effect of countless generations of cultural humus laid upon a landscape of superb natural beauty. Recent man-made additions of coniferous woodlands, reservoirs (mainly above Nidderdale), together with the growing scars of limestone quarrying in Ribblesdale, Wharfedale, and lower Wensleydale, have less deleterious effects on the landscape than the disfiguring, disproportionate but permitted structures of new, large agricultural buildings which are outside the planning control of the National Park Committee.

The basic objectives of the National Park Committee, designated in 1954, can conveniently be summarised:

1. To see that the landscape evolves without losing its natural beauty.
2. To enhance the landscape.
3. To give full consideration to local interests.
4. To promote better understanding between town and country.
5. To enable visitors to enjoy the natural beauty.
6. To ensure that recreational activities are compatible and do not harm the natural beauty.

Generally, conservation has priority over recreation. At the same time the needs of agriculture have to be balanced against the claims of conservation. Upland farming depends heavily on public subsidies and before capital grants are paid to farmers for land improvements they are expected to consult the National Park Committee to show that regard has been taken concerning implications for conservation and public enjoyment.

The National Park Committee now offers a wide service with free advice and financial assistance towards certain types of forestry, especially to encourage farmers and landowners to plant locally native or traditional trees, and for management of existing broadleaved amenity woodlands. Grants are also available to cover the cost of repairing boundaries to woods, providing new fencing, to buy and plant trees, and to control rabbits.

But so far as the visiting public are concerned the likeliest impact made by the National Park Committee is through its Information Centres and Warden service. A separate contribution details the Centres (see page 59); six full-time Wardens, many field-workers, and a large number of volunteer helpers work throughout the year to maintain 1000 miles of public footpaths and bridleways, waymarking wherever possible, repairing stiles and footbridges, and supervising an agreed programme of conservation projects, in which almost all the work is done by volunteer groups. All of this represents hundreds of man-hours directed towards the dual aims of conservation and public enjoyment, yet bearing in mind at all times that the area is the work-place for thousands of people who live there. For them, and the countless visitors who are welcomed, the Yorkshire Dales is a particular paradise.

Limestone Scenery

Long scars of bare white rock are the unmistakable mark of limestone stamped on the landscape of the Yorkshire Dales. More than any other rock, limestone imposes its own character on the scenery – with its scars, crags, gorges, sinkholes and caves. It is these features which create such a trademark for the Yorkshire Dales, particularly in the southern part of the Park, where the Great Scar Limestone dominates the country around Malham and Ingleborough, creating what is known as a karst landscape.

Tropical sea

It was therefore a lucky break within the geological record that, 330 million years ago, the Western Yorkshire area was a shallow tropical sea. The ancient slates of that sea floor can be seen beneath the Great Scar Limestone in Ribblesdale, or half way down the Thornton Force waterfall at Ingleton. But it was in the sea that millions of animals lived and died, leaving their broken shells to build up the limestone layers. The Great Scar Limestone was solidified when it was buried beneath a sequence of sandstones, limestones and shales which were deposited by muddy rivers draining into the ancient sea. These became the Yoredale Series of rocks, now forming the summit plinths of the Three Peaks (Ingleborough, Pen-y-ghent and Whernside), and into which are also carved all the northern Dales – they were christened with the ancient name for Wensleydale. The thin Yoredale limestones can hardly dominate the landscape, but they form the caprocks at many of the waterfalls and also define the valley side rock terraces, both of which characterise the northern Dales.

Fractured rock

Massive earth movements later folded and fractured all the rocks and also uplifted them to form the core of the Pennines. The movements created the joints, so conspicuous on any of the limestone plateaux, and displaced the rocks on some massive faults. Giggleswick Scar lies on the

Kilnsey Crag, an unspoilt limestone cliff

most obvious of the famous Craven Faults; the fault line is traced by the A65 road west of Settle, where limestone crags rise high on the north side but the same rock lies buried deep beneath younger sandstones just across the road. The fractures also provided pathways for hot fluids migrating through the rock when it was deeply buried; these deposited the minerals of lead, zinc and barium which miners have since torn from the long thin veins in the limestone, notably beneath Grassington Moor and the Swaledale area.

The carving of the landscape

A much later stage in the geological history of the Yorkshire Dales was the carving of the landscape, mostly by rivers and glaciers within the last million years or so. At times, ice covered the entire Dales area – it was probably a kilometre thick in places – but the ice sheets expanded and waned a number of times in response to the climatic changes. Hills and valleys were moulded successively by rivers and glaciers, but a vital aspect of the erosion was when glaciers flowed in the confines of the valleys, opening them out to create the broad floors and steep sides which so characterise the Dales.

The broad features of the landscape were very much fashioned by the glaciers, but the character of the limestone dominates the details of the scenery. Along the flanks of many of the Dales, the limestone beds stand proud as long lines of bare white crags and scars. Twistleton Scars and Raven Scar along opposite sides of Chapel-le-Dale are among the finest. Their rock faces were plucked clean by the passing glaciers and have survived since the end of the Ice Age due firstly to the strength of the limestone and secondly to its complete solution in rainwater so that no debris remains to form a soil. Most of the scars clearly relate to the limestone bedding but some are on a larger scale. Just south of the confluence of the Wharfedale and Littondale glaciers, a rock spur was trimmed right back to form Kilnsey Crag, a spectacular overhanging limestone face.

Limestone pavements

High above the staircase of scars, the glaciers once also overrode the broad plateaux, and there the combination of ice and limestone has excelled. The limestone pavements of Yorkshire are unforgettable. During the last Ice Age, 15,000 years ago, glaciers scoured the limestone clean, and since then rainwater has slowly eaten into the rock. It has cut little solution runnels across the slabs, and has opened the fractures into wide rounded rifts; these are known as grikes, and the blocks between are called clints. On the famous pavement at the top of Malham Cove, the numerous runnels and grikes create a highly dissected surface, in total contrast to the pavements of north-western Ingleborough which have much broader clints with widely spaced runnels. Even more impressive is the southern spur of Whernside, Scales Moor, where huge expanses of pavement are devoid of vegetation.

The effects of rainwater

The solutional features of the pavements exist because the limestone is dissolved by rainwater, though of course extremely slowly. The same process permits underground drainage of the

The precipitous face of Malham Cove (right)

karst country. Water gets into the narrow joints of any rock, but moves so slowly that it can only enlarge the fractures by chemical solution. Limestone is therefore the only common rock where fractures are opened up, eventually to become caves, on a scale adequate to absorb all surface drainage. So a characteristic of the limestone hills is the vast number of sinkholes – which may be anything from tiny fissures taking just seepage water, to gaping holes swallowing large streams. Particularly common in the Dales are shakeholes – conical depressions 2–20m across which pockmark the sheets of glacial boulder clay overlying the limestone. They have formed as the sediment has been washed down into the open limestone fissures below: analogies with an egg-timer are most appropriate. There are thousands of them in the Dales, and perhaps those on the southern slopes of Ingleborough are among the finest.

Caves and potholes
Streams commonly sink into larger openings – potholes if they are vertical shafts or caves if they are closer to horizontal. These are some of the highlights of the Dales landscapes. Most famous is Gaping Gill, high on south-eastern Ingleborough, where Fell Beck plummets into darkness, falling 110m down a shaft 10m across which opens into a massive chamber down below. A more impressive view from the surface is provided by Alum Pot, on the north-eastern slopes of Ingleborough. It is a huge rift in the hillside, long enough and wide enough to see right down past the rock ledges to the floor 60m below. Today little water flows down it, as the larger stream which formed the pothole now sinks further back up the hill where it has found a new underground route.

The Butter Tubs
A group of potholes called the Butter Tubs are well known because of their roadside location on the pass from Wensleydale to Swaledale north of Hawes. Unlike the bold rift of Alum Pot, they are irregular shaped shafts fluted where their walls have been cut back by small streams draining from the nearby peat haggs. Only 20m deep, they cut almost the full thickness of a thin Yoredale limestone. Between these extremes of size and shape, there are hundreds of potholes on the high slopes of the Yorkshire hills – each carved by its own stream, each different, and each unique to limestone.

Cave streams
All the water that sinks into the limestone eventually has to return to daylight. Collecting underground into a series of larger cave streams, most of it emerges from just a handful of risings; in the Three Peaks area there are one or two in the floor of each main valley. The water may pour from an open cave mouth, such as Clapham Beck Head where the Gaping Gill water rediscovers the open air on the south side of Ingleborough. Alternatively the rising may be a dark, still pool, like Keld Head just below the road in Kingsdale, where a powerful river rises silently from a submerged cave.

Between the sinkholes and the risings lie the caves – the underground arteries which have captured the natural drainage. They all started life as narrow fissures in the limestone, but the flow of

Top: Entering Rumbling Hole, Leck Fell
Bottom: The effects of water erosion

water over tens of thousands of years has enlarged them into wide open tunnels. The simplest form of cave is a single streamway with long stretches of gently descending passage interrupted by vertical shafts where a joint has guided the water down to greater depths. Gaping Gill is the prime example of a shaft, though on an uncharacteristically large scale, and the passage in the White Scar show cave, at Ingleton, is a typical active streamway. A single stream cascades into Calf Holes, beside the Pennine Way above Ribblesdale, and emerges from Browgill Cave just 500m away. This is a complete cave system in miniature, but even smaller is God's Bridge further down the same stream, where the water ducks underground for just ten metres, finding a bedding plane which it follows back to the hillside.

Underground mazes
Most caves are much more complex. Perhaps a dozen sinking streams may unite underground in a single cave river, to create a rambling, branching system. Yet more complication is added by the dimension of depth. Water always tries to find the lowest route through the limestone, and over time it progressively abandons passages at higher

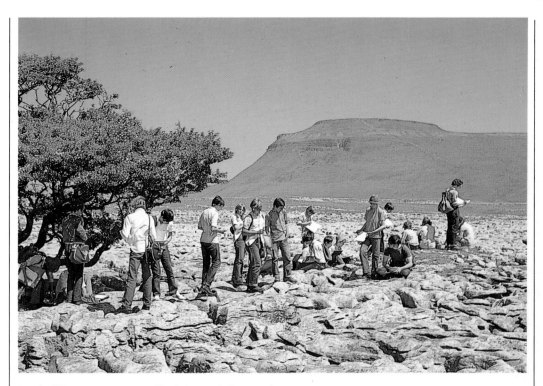

levels. The tourist section of Ingleborough Cave is a tunnel once used by the Gaping Gill drainage, but it is now almost dry as today's water flows in a younger parallel stream cave at a lower level. Where a series of tributary stream caves cut down through a host of old abandoned tunnels, the result can be a gigantic three dimensional maze. Under the western edge of the limestone, north of Ingleton, the Ease Gill Cave System has nearly 50km of interconnected passages of all sorts and sizes. There are narrow twisting fissures, and sweeping tunnels 15m high and wide; there are huge silent caverns, and roaring waterfall shafts; and there are beautiful displays of stalactites and stalagmites where dripwater has redeposited some of the dissolved limestone as sparkling white calcite.

Because the drainage is underground, much of the surface maybe dry; even major valleys can be streamless. Kingsdale was largely cut by Ice Age glaciers, but the modern stream bypasses it through a long cave system under its western flank. Only in flood does the main beck carry too much water to be absorbed by the debris-choked sinkholes at the edge of the limestone; then the channel (artificially straightened) down the floor of Kingsdale carries a short-lived torrent of floodwater. Upper Littondale also has a cave route which in dry weather can take all the drainage; it leaves a streambed of dry rock through Litton village.

Effects of the Ice Age
A permanently dry valley extends from Gaping Gill down through the gorge of Trow Gill into the upper end of Clapdale. Its size and shape tell that it is not of glacial origin but was cut by a small river. During the Ice Ages there were times when there was no immediate ice cover, but the ground was deep frozen and the existing caves were blocked by ice. Meltwater from snowfields and nearby glaciers therefore flowed on the surface of the limestone, and cut the valley, deepening into a gorge on the steeper gradient down through Trow

A field study party examines the limestone pavement at Ingleborough

Gill. Since the climate has improved, the limestone has lost its seal of ice, the drainage has returned underground, and the valley has been left dry.

Meltwater streams
These meltwater streams were largely responsible for cutting so many of the dry valleys and gorges in the Dales limestone country. The most spectacular results are found at Malham. Fed from dying ice on the Malham Tarn upland, two major meltwater rivers flowed south, and cascaded off the edge of the limestone plateau along the fault line through Malham village. The western river cut the splendid Watlowes valley, now dry, and at the edge of the plateau dropped over a massive waterfall which cut back to form a vertical face in the limestone. That is at least part of the story behind the dramatic 70m high cliff of Malham Cove, though the great width of the Cove suggests that ice may also have played a role in a rather more complex history. Two kilometres to the east, the second river cut the Gordale valley. At the edge of the plateau it did not form a single waterfall, but instead used the steeper gradient and a series of cascades to incise itself into a narrow gorge. Gordale Scar is a monumental feature with its cliffs towering 100m above the shadowy depths; within it a natural arch is a remnant of cave passage revealed when the gorge cut down into it. The stream through Gordale today is tiny compared to the torrent which must have cut the gorge, and now that most of the water is underground the cliffs stand uneroded as a reminder of those bygone events.

The Gordale cliffs and the Scales Moor pavements may have been cut by water and ice, but both only exist because the rock is limestone. The same applies to the potholes and caves, and they have all combined to develop the unmistakable character of the Yorkshire Dales landscape.

A Day in the Life of a Dalesman

Clark Stones has spent most of his life as a farmer in the Upper Dales. Conditions are often testing and sometimes cruel

Daybreak

Arkengarthdale – 'Ark'nd'l' to the natives – daybreak, early April. . . . As he fought off lingering sleep farmer Clark Stones was aware that the long winter sequence of silent dawns was now interrupted by a symphony of sounds – blackbirds staking territorial claims, lapwings piping impertinent wolf-whistles, curlews bubbling in composed jubilation – the avian prelude to summer. Nevertheless last night's cloudless skies and still dank air had warned him of a hard frost to threaten any lamb improvidently born of darkness on the hillsides.

His thoughts floated back to the evening's final rounds and the pathetic near-strangled lamb he had delivered from a neighbour's exhausted ewe. It was lucky he had been able to manipulate its legs and wrest it from its fateful predicament – head out, but one foreleg crooked preventing its dropping. He had taken it down with its dam to a protective straw-filled barn, but he knew by its bloated discoloured face that its chances were slim. At such times care and compassion over-rule all other considerations.

In the short space it takes to tumble into clothes and gulp a hasty cup of tea, he was back in the fields right up to the moor's edge, searching every wall corner or hidden gully for ewes in difficult labour or lambs in need of assistance. Throughout, his practised eye subconsciously scanned the containing drystone walls for gaps that might tempt the inquisitive ewes to stray.

Like his father and grandfather who farmed before him, Clark Stones was born and bred in the dale. From the village school he earned a grammar school place at Richmond where, because of Arkengarthdale's remoteness, he had to be a boarder. A natural athlete, he played an active part in all sports, laying the foundations for future satisfaction and success in the field, particularly in cricket and rugby.

After university in Scotland, two years' National Service with the Royal Engineers allowed further indulgence of his sporting inclinations, highlighted when he refused selection for a commission to spend three months with his regiment on intensive ski-training in Germany. A year with the Forestry Commission in Argyllshire allowed a continuance of his favourite sports, cricket, rugby and ski-ing, extended at this time to include water-ski-ing on the sea lochs. He later resigned to join his father and learn the craft of farming at Pepper Hall Farm in Arkengarthdale. By the time he was thirty the farm was made over to him, although his father continued to assist in semi-retirement for another twelve years.

Married to an equally active, sporting and hard-working wife, Greta, he has two teenage sons. Robert, the eldest, works on a nearby farm and follows a day-release course in agriculture at a local college. Later he hopes to spend a couple of years in the United States, after which the farm will be open, if he wishes, to ease him into ownership. Philip, the youngest, boards at Barnard Castle School. His future is deliberately undetermined. Like their parents, the boys are enthusiastic skiers, both of a calibre approaching international standard. They also share an enthusiasm for motor-cycle scrambling, the rugged terrain of much of the home farm being ideally suited for its pursuit.

Clark hung up his rugby boots a few years ago after considerable service to Darlington Rugby Union Football Club. His cricketing interests, apart from a rare deputising appearance on the field, concentrate now on the chairmanship of Reeth Cricket Club. But the family addiction to ski-ing persists, often to the extent of precipitating a hard 250 mile overnight drive to Glenshee to participate in downhill races, followed by an immediate exhausted return to the ever demanding livestock.

His early round of the sheep completed, Clark's attention had now to be concentrated on the cattle, especially the milkers. The Dairy Crest's blue and white tanker would call at 10.30 am, by which time not only had 17 cows to be milked, but the milk had to be cooled to below 40F before it could be taken.

Nine cows were led into the milking parlour, haltered, and given water and food to settle them. Immaculate in long white coat, Clark sensitively washed down each cow before attaching its individual milker. The cows appeared to enjoy the experience, while the farm cats looked on in anticipation of their share. Farm cats are maintained principally to keep down vermin. Since they hunt for pleasure, not for food, and the healthiest make the best hunters, their ration is neither grudged nor stinted.

The nine having been milked and the milk decanted into the cooler in the nearby dairy, silage had to be led by tractor from the outside clamp to circular feeding stalls. The milked cows were put to them to feed while the remaining eight milkers were brought into the parlour from their loose housing for a repeat performance.

Mid morning

Having already accomplished the equivalent of a townsman's half-day's work, it was now time for a hearty traditional breakfast, a chance to skim the contents of the ominous buff envelopes brought by the postman, and the opportunity to update Greta on the lambing situation. After all, she might at any time be called upon to take in to nurse and feed some weakling lamb or one rejected by its mother. In any case, on a one-man farm, it is only prudent that the farmer's wife is fully acquainted with all aspects of its operation in the dreaded event of an unforeseen emergency.

No time to linger after breakfast. A bucketful of concentrates fed to the breeding ewes in an in-bye meadow offered the opportunity for a precautionary inspection of those immediately due to drop their lambs. Their unaccustomed trot to their feed flushed a startled snipe into typical zig-zag flight, while a flash of white along the wall top betrayed the season's first wheatear, newly arrived from far off tropical Africa.

Near the congregated ewes Clark noticed a wet patch – probably a fractured field drain – and made a mental note to investigate further in less pressured times. There were other peaty patches in the steeply sloping field, some badly poached by heavy-footed cattle in last year's damp late autumn. But there was also a broad dark trampled swath angled down the field to a corner near the village – the tell-tale legacy of a party of fifty schoolchildren and their transgressing teachers – only a stone's throw from a public right of way along a dry metalled track! With only fifty-five acres of harvestable grass for essential winter fodder and the prohibitive cost of bought-in substitutes, such damage could, in hard times, have critical consequences. Our Dalesman reflected on the deed with philosophical calm when others might, with cause, have been roused to angry protestation.

Feeding the ewes and young lambs

Back at the big barn the black and white Friesian bull and some fifty young or in-calf followers were beginning to voice a peevish demand for food and attention. Hay and concentrates were issued in measured quantities, straw was laid, and a considerate, educated eye measured their health and appearance, each and every one a distinctive individual.

The rumble of the milk tanker drew Clark to assist at the dairy. Drivers are in such a continual hurry to meet manufacturing deadlines at the dairy in Northallerton that any assistance is welcomed. The produce of each herd is regularly examined for milk-fat and bacteriological content, demanding close attention to hygiene and diet. The consequences of electrical breakdown hindering the cooling process, or of roads impassable through snowstorm or flash flood preventing collection might plague uneasier minds, but lifelong experience with the animals and the elements induces in the Dales farmer a patience and inner calm greatly to be envied.

Midday

The next task was the inescapable mucking out of the milking parlour by the traditional shovel and barrow, followed by scraping out the loose house by tractor, the manure being deposited directly into the muck spreader. Fresh straw was then spread, and the stock brought in again. The barley straw is brought from a lowland farm at Eppleby, some twenty miles distant to the north-east, coincidentally the object of the next assignment.

The unpredictable climate of the dale, the inhospitable altitude of the farm straddling the 1000 foot contour, and the uncompromising nature of the land – steep, peaty, and pocked with lead-impregnated debris from former lead mining – preclude the over-wintering of the whole flock at Pepper Hall Farm. So for five winter months each year the hoggs (last year's lambs) are taken to kinder pastures. A former school-fellow and rugby team-mate who farms at Eppleby acts as host to about fifty hoggs, mostly gimmers (females), as well as providing the bedding straw. Yesterday Clark drove over to collect half of them. Now he could bring back the remainder.

The family's devotion to ski-ing had dictated the rejection of the ubiquitous Land Rover in favour of an estate car in which the children could sleep on the long journeys to and from the Scottish ski slopes. The trailer was securely attached and Fly, the oldest and most reliable of the four sheep dogs, leapt willingly inside. Down the track to the old mining village of Langthwaite, up past the CB Inn, Clark turned right on to the historic Stang road – used certainly in Roman times, and probably for centuries before.

The steep one-in-four ascent invoked recollection of desperate experience with tractor and straw-loaded trailer travelling downhill. The risk of a tractor running out of control on the steep hillsides of the dale is always in the minds of the farmers, many of whom have been fortunate to survive overturning or collision. Broad bands of uprooted conifers in the Stang Forest offered stark reminders of the severe gales that rattled the area in January leaving a wake of fallen trees, broken walls, and perforated roofs. The A66 – the Roman 'Street' across Stainmore – was beginning to feel the weight of the early visitor.

The hoggs, gently driven into the trailer at Eppleby, had a healthy, well-fed appearance. One wether (male) hogg had died, and a gimmer had ripped off an entangled horn, but otherwise their stay had brought great benefit. The return journey, through Richmond to avoid the dreaded descent of the Stang with such a heavy load, was taken at a cautious speed.

Back at the farm they were unloaded and driven into a disused farm building along with yesterday's batch, to await drenching and marking before release on to the moor.

Clark had now put in the equivalent of many a townsman's full working day, and it was time to pause for a well-earned lunch.

The fifty hoggs were penned in the large doorless kitchen of the old Low Lockhouse Farm (datestone 1781), several adopting strategic stances on the raised central hearth or the flanking upper recesses below an embracing three-arched chimney breast. All pure Swaledales, the majority were gimmer hoggs. Towards the end of the year the weakest would be sold off at Hawes Auction Mart, leaving the healthiest forty to maintain the flock's breeding stock. They now had to be prepared for the moor.

Clark inspects the horns of each tup

Each in turn was captured and, firmly grasped between the farmer's knees, dosed through the mouth with a potion to eradicate flukes and other internal infections. There followed a careful inspection of each animal, revealing in two cases horns growing into the flesh just below the eyes. These had to be carefully pruned with a hacksaw. All were stripe-marked with rud (red dye) over the shoulders – the farm's distinctive livery.

Drenching and marking accomplished, the hoggs were driven by the dogs up through the fields to the moor wall. Once through the gate they were left to pick their individual ways to their traditional 'heafs'. These are the parts of the moor where generation after generation of whole families of sheep have assumed almost exclusive grazing territories to which they always return after removal or dispersal. This ancient system of moorland sheep management is helpful because they learn the locations of the choicest grazing patches and sheltered hollows, but also build up immunity to indigenous infestations. Additionally, and of crucial importance on this particular piece of open moorland, they have learnt to avoid the fatal vegetation of the lead spoil heaps that in recent times have claimed the lives of three heifers (young cows).

Here, dark mysterious tunnels, some miles in length, drain subterranean water from old lead workings and untold caves; strange ruins and mountains of mine waste create fantastic landscapes; while more recent quarrying of dark grey marble-like chert has left vast carpets of scree-like debris to deface the heathery hillsides. All seem havens for the resurgent rabbits that mercifully for the farmers' sake have been dramatically culled by a long cold winter.

The tractor is used for a variety of tasks

From the fellside Clark returned through the pastures to check again on the lambing ewes, to supplement their diet with hay and concentrates, and to reassure himself on their well-being. On the banks of a gurgling beck the first gold coltsfoot flashed a friendly greeting, while in the water the lush watercress and the spreading brooklime promised an early splash of colour. The customary herons were not to be seen. Perhaps they had started to build their nests.

The hazy sun was beginning to sink towards the high hilly horizons, but there was still much that needed attention. The morning's routine of milking, fothering, mucking out and strawing was all to be repeated, as it was on the other 364 days a year. Young calves in outlying byres demanded food and water. Last night's half-strangled lamb had to be checked – it was now miraculously none the worse for its unhappy entrance into the world. And a score of other minor chores could be put off no longer.

Clark checks the udders of a cow that has recently dropped its calf

Dusk

High tea afforded a relaxing interlude, but with Robert now back from his daily employment, there was still an hour or so of daylight for him to help his father rebuild a section of fallen wall. Once damaged, early repair is essential not only to retain the sheep, but also to prevent great lengths falling like toppling dominoes. For though they may not be as old as the hills, many extend back over several centuries, and with care will last as long again.

Repairing a section of drystone wall

Their mortarless construction follows the age-old principle of a firm broad footing (foundation) and two converging walls erected in overlapping courses, the centre packed with small stones, tied intermediately with 'troughs' (through or tie stones spanning the full width of the wall and sometimes extruding at the faces), built up to about five feet then finished with top stones or cap stones, often set on end for extra stability. The stones of clumsily irregular shapes and sizes require skilful selection and placement, making what may appear to be a fairly simple and straightforward process a matter of real craftsmanship, if not a true art form. The walls are as much an integral part of landscape and heritage as man himself, with his animals the architect and preserver of the present scenario.

The walling gave Clark and Robert a chance to discuss their days' transactions and the conditions of the livestock, until too soon they realised that encroaching darkness obliged a final round of the fields with the breeding ewes.

Evening

Their torchlight return to the farmhouse, to collapse into comfortable armchairs to contemplate the state of the farm, or at the insistence of the inevitable television the state of the nation, was not necessarily the end of the working day. With a family of over 200 animals, who knew what calls or crises might suddenly be thrust upon them, even in the still, small hours?

Justifiably, after some fifteen hours of hard manual outdoor work and the ever-present weight of all his responsibilities, Clark decided to put off once again those unending returns for the nine-to-five men from the ministry and the Inland Revenue. Perhaps half an hour on the piano and a few choruses from Mendelssohn's *Elijah* might be more conducive to a quiet night.

Arkil, after whose garth (enclosure) the dale is named, was the son of Gospatric the Viking pre-conquest landowner. When the Conqueror made over the estates to Alan, Earl of Richmond, it was significant that he appointed the same Robert Arkil his head forester. One is tempted to consider whether Arkil's position was changed in any way, and if he did not continue in his original position of influence and social standing. His modest dignity, his strength and resilience, his inspiration of trust and a courteous refusal to scrape to usurped authority, are qualities that have been passed down and preserved in modern times in the character of the authentic Dalesman.

Clark Stones is a man of such qualities, graced to be, as Shelley wrote of Hunt, 'one of those happy souls which are the salt of the earth'. In hands like these, with pride and concern for the heritage he has become part of, the nation can rest assured that at least the little part of England that falls within his stewardship will be lovingly preserved.

In a rare quiet moment Clark finds time to survey the beauty of his surroundings

Recreation in the Dales

The hills and dales of north-west Yorkshire make a magnificent backdrop for recreation, whether to the athlete bent on strenuous physical exertion, or to the gently strolling country-lover.

A thousand-plus miles of well-defined public paths and ancient tracks beside sparkling streams and waterfalls, through meadows dotted with wild flowers and fragrant upland pastures, or even on the wildest hagg-pocked moorlands evoke feelings of tranquillity not often achieved in 20th-century life.

Pathfinding

Many visitors to the Dales, conscious that most of the land is privately owned, are anxious about trespass and interference with and by livestock. Respect for other people's property and privacy is right and proper, but this must not inhibit your rightful enjoyment of the countryside which warmhearted Dalesfolk, proud of their heritage, are pleased to share with you.

Throughout the area is a comprehensive network of public footpaths indicated by fingerposts and symbols, if not by visible evidence on the ground. Footpaths are further identified by yellow discs or arrows on gateposts and stiles, and on walls or buildings where there is a possibility of going astray. Bridleways, identified by larger blue discs or patches, are open to pedestrians, but also to horse riders and cyclists.

Using Ordnance Survey maps

All these paths and bridleways, as well as roads used as public paths, are indicated in red on the maps in this book, and on all the other *Landranger* maps of the Ordnance Survey. They are shown by broken green lines on the 1:25000 *Outdoor Leisure* maps and on the 1:25000 *Pathfinder* series, which also include for additional definition all field boundaries and further details of local features and facilities. These three Ordnance Survey map series help not only to find one's way around but, because of all the information they display, simplify holiday planning without the fear of overlooking places and features of special interest.

Guided walks

For many visitors the most rewarding introduction to the area will be through the National Park's comprehensive programme of guided walks led by local people with intimate knowledge and infinite enthusiasm for the countryside in which they live.

These gentle afternoon walks averaging three to four miles in distance and up to three hours in duration are well within the capabilities of most people. They usually have a central theme such as flowers, birds, farming, local history, geology and lead mining, but embrace consideration of the whole environment. Of particular interest to children, a number of farm visits and sheep dog demonstrations are made along the way.

Birdwatching at Malham Tarn

Details of the walks are available at the National Park Information Centres or in *The Visitor*, the National Park's free newspaper that also contains articles about the heritage and traditions of the Yorkshire Dales and the people who live and work in them.

'Dales Rail' guided walks
Those whose holidays encompass the first weekend of every month from May to October will have the unique opportunity of combining a ride along the country's most spectacular railway – the controversial Settle–Carlisle line – with the choice of up to a dozen free guided walks from an easy six miles to a strenuous twenty. The 'Dales Rail' service, set up in 1975 under the joint organisation of the Yorkshire Dales National Park, the West Yorkshire Passenger Transport Executive and British Rail, offers to people from West Yorkshire, Lancashire and North Cumbria, access to the Dales and opportunities for countryside recreation otherwise denied since the closure of the line to local traffic in 1970.

Details of the walks and the times of trains and connecting buses are available from the Yorkshire Dales National Park, Bainbridge, Leyburn, North Yorkshire. Dales people and visitors may also use the service for day outings to Carlisle, Leeds and Bradford.

Self-guided walks
For those who find map-reading a mystery or a distraction several options present themselves. The simplest is a series of well-defined walks or nature trails, some of which are on private land (necessitating the payment of a small entrance fee). They include Hardraw Force in Wensleydale, The Malham Tarn Nature Trail, The Reginald Farrer Nature Trail from Clapham, and the Ingleton Waterfalls Trail. Most have descriptive leaflets, some of which are published by the National Park. This book includes 16 easy-to-follow, circular walks specially geared to family groups who want to spend a day or so exploring the Dales at their own pace. In addition the National Park also publishes an increasing range of low-cost self-guided walk leaflets that explain simply and clearly the directions to be taken, and indicate and interpret points of interest to look out for. These are available at any of the National Park Centres.

Famous footpaths
The Dales Way – from Ilkley to Bowness – is classified as a 'Recreational Path' by the Countryside Commission. To cross the northern dales A Wainwright's *A Coast to Coast Walk* is popular and the prestigious Pennine Way, which is a designated 'Long Distance Footpath' is described in detail on pages 26–30.

The Three Peaks
The ultimate challenge for walkers in the Yorkshire Dales is the demanding 22-mile switchback plod over the summits of Pen-y-ghent, Whernside and Ingleborough. Its completion within twelve hours (average eight hours) qualifies for membership of The Three Peaks of Yorkshire Club based at Pen-y-ghent Café, Horton in Ribblesdale, Settle, North Yorkshire. The walk is detailed in *Walks in the Limestone Country* by A Wainwright, *Yorkshire's Three Peaks* by The Dalesman, and *The Three Peaks Map and Guide* by

Crossing the finishing line of the Mountain Marathon, Howgill Fells

Stiles Publications. Potential walkers should be warned that severely adverse weather and underfoot conditions can combine at short notice to make this a punishing endurance or even survival test.

Visitors should recognise that many public footpaths cross pastures and meadows whose crops are critical to the whole agricultural economy. Within the Yorkshire Dales where soils, altitude and climate militate against arable farming, the total emphasis is on grass production. The grass, whether as permanent year-round sustenance or in hay and silage as vital winter feed, is used to build up sturdy young sheep and cattle to be fattened for the table on lowland farms, or to sustain the dairy products for which the Dales are so famous. Isaiah said 'All flesh is grass', but here in the Dales one could equally say 'All grass is flesh'.

It is therefore not only courteous but also provident to keep crop damage to the minimum by walking in single file across enclosed pastures.

Livestock
The law now permits farmers to graze certain breeds of beef bulls with cows or heifers in fields crossed by public footpaths. Provided they are not provoked and given a wide berth, these animals will regard you with nothing more than curiosity. It cannot be over stressed, however, that all animals should be treated with respect, but the solitary black and white dairy bull should be avoided at all costs. After calving, some cows can become aggressive if you place yourself between them and their calf.

All animals, including humans, are naturally curious, and so you can expect your gazes to be reciprocated. But they are also easily excited, and therefore dogs should be kept on leads at all times, and restrained from provoking livestock by barking or lunging at them. This is equally important with sheep and lambs, and it is well to remember that if chased, pregnant cows and sheep can easily miscarry.

Farmers complain with justification about the problems created by the occasional careless visitor failing to secure gates after them. The mixing of different farmers' stock, disruption of cropping regimes, premature or unwanted mating, spread of infection, straying on to highways with consequent danger both to traffic and to the animals: these are just a few of the possible consequences of a momentary lapse of concentration or consideration. So please, fasten all gates securely behind you.

A group of potholers discuss tactics at the mouth of Ingleborough Cave

Caves and potholes

From Nidderdale in the east to Barbondale in the west no less than 200km of natural underground drainage channels have been explored and surveyed. With many more awaiting discovery, the area can justifiably be called 'The Cave District'.

To some, the words caves and potholes conjure up thoughts of dangerous places fit only for savage beasts or malevolent spirits. To others they represent mystery and wonder, challenge and adventure, their exploration a source of excitement.

The sport of caving or potholing calls upon advanced skills. Physically very demanding and beset with potential dangers like unexpected shafts, rockfalls and sudden flooding, it is one to be contemplated only under expert tuition. But in the Yorkshire Dales the curious and adventurous can meet their aspirations by a simple progression.

Show caves

Within the National Park are three show caves where visitors are given conducted tours along comfortable illuminated passages. The White Scar Cave at Ingleton with its stream, its spectacular waterfalls, its stalactites and stalagmites and displaying clearly the geological unconformity of the district, makes an interesting appetiser, even for the disabled in wheelchairs.

Stump Cross Caverns at Greenhow Hill between Grassington and Pateley Bridge extends the experience by the inclusion of two new dimensions: its one-time occupation by wolverine, bison, fox and reindeer proved by the finds of fossilised bones; and the intrusive workings of centuries of lead miners. Stump Cross guides complete their tours with a compelling colour video film by Sid Perou on the inner recesses of the caverns and the caving techniques used to explore them. Both White Scar and Stump Cross offer free parking and restaurant facilities.

Ingleborough Cave is a pleasant mile and a half walk up Clapdale from the Clapham National Park Centre and car park. Arguably the most natural of the show caves it features stalactites, stalagmites, the active growth of tufa, and other interesting geological features including large fossils in the cave walls. Of particular interest to many are the albino shrimps, worms and insect larvae in the stream and pools. Recently, the long-anticipated breakthrough has been made between this system and that of Gaping Gill, a mile further up the dale.

An intrepid potholer descends into the abyss

Gaping Gill

Gaping Gill is the country's most spectacular pothole falling sheerly from an awesome oval 'gape' 20m by 10m across down to Britain's largest chamber – about the size of York Minster – some 104m below. Impressive from above, the chamber is breathtaking from below with water cascading all the way down to sink mysteriously into the floor to follow deeper explored passages that emerge in Ingleborough Cave. For the ten days preceding Spring and August Bank Holidays the Craven and Bradford Pothole Clubs erect a winch at the mouth to permit the public to descend and share in its wonders.

For the walker a range of caves of reasonable access and safety exist throughout the area, of which the most popular are the historic Victoria and Attermire Caves, approached from Settle or Langcliffe, and Yorda's Cave in Kingsdale. Accounts of such caves and how to approach them are found in A Wainwright's *Walks in Limestone Country* and his *Walks in the Howgill Fells*.

Caving instruction

The Whernside National Caving Training Centre, operated by the Yorkshire Dales National Park, mounts a wide range of caving courses throughout the year. One of its most popular offerings is a one-day introductory caving course that features a morning of talks, slide shows and demonstration followed by an afternoon's guided exploration in a cave. Experienced cavers of all grades can select from a wide range of weekend, five-day or one week courses. Fell-walking, natural history, bird-watching, canoeing and multi-activity courses are also available, of which the canoeing and bird-watching courses are offered as one-day options. Full particulars are obtainable from Whernside Cave and Fell Centre, Dent, Sedbergh, Cumbria LA10 5RE, *tel* Dent (05875) 213, location: OS map reference SD 725858.

Mineral and stone mines

Almost since time began man has been mining the Dales for minerals and stone. Lead mining, its most profitable venture, was concentrated in two major fields, from Grassington Moor to Greenhow Hill, and in North Swaledale bestraddling Arkengarthdale. In these areas in particular, extensive evidence of former burrowings and burnings is revealed by tailings (spoil heaps), bell pits, adits and levels (tunnels), watercourses and reservoirs, crushing and smelt mills and tunnel-like flues extending up steep hillsides. Elsewhere shafts of old copper, calamine (zinc) and coal mines, and the tunnels of the Wensleydale slate mines invite the attention of the curious. It must be emphasised that unlike the natural caves and potholes of the limestone areas, these old man-made passages are most unsafe and should not be entered at any cost. Artefacts and implements, rock samples and pictures of their former operation are now well represented in folk museums like Hawes and Grassington, but especially at the Mines Museum at Earby, south of Skipton. Their history is well documented by local authors A Raistrick and R T Clough, and in the journals of the Northern Mine Research Society, South Anston, Sheffield.

Hawes underground stone mine

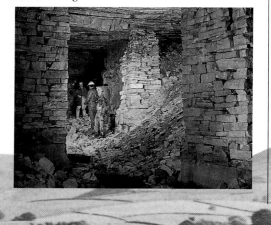

Cycling

An ideal way to explore the picturesque villages and the ancient wandering lanes of the valleys is by cycle. The leisurely self-dictated pace, the constant opportunity to stop and stare whenever the inclination moves, and the direct impact of the countryside – the sights, the scents and the sounds – combine to generate a sense of well-being and an empathy with one's surroundings.

To reach another dale or some high vantage point may necessitate a bit of uphill pushing, but the subsequent rewards of splendid panoramic views and the exhilarating downhill coast will more than compensate. Cycles may be hired from

Hawes trotting race, where galloping is strictly against the rules

the Ropeworks in Hawes, and from a number of shops in the larger towns.

Pony trekking

Equally rewarding for the less energetic or the lover of animals is to commune with the countryside on the back of a well-schooled Dales pony. Four centres offer one-hour, half-day and full day treks, as well as tuition and longer trails. Details of these are given in the Directory (p68).

Swimming

The Dales abound with becks and streams which can be fun for children to splash around in, though few offer safe pools deep or calm enough for swimming. Exceptions may be found in the lower reaches of the southern sector, as at Bolton Abbey in Wharfedale or Stainforth Force in Ribblesdale, but even these can be dangerous in spate or unhealthy in drought. Council-maintained swimming pools of very high standard exist at Skipton, Settle, Ingleton, Threshfield and Richmond.

Angling

The rivers and becks afford excellent opportunities in their appropriate seasons for trout and grayling fishing. Of particular interest to the disabled is the facility at Widdale Beck near Hawes for wheelchair anglers. However in this area, as well as one or two others, no fishing is allowed on Sundays. Trout fishing is also available at a number of reservoirs, and on a few privately-owned lakes like Malham Tarn and Semer Water, which offer the additional opportunity of catching perch. Fly fishing for rainbow trout is available at Kilnsey Park in Wharfedale. On the southern fringe of the National Park, the Leeds to Liverpool Canal offers the opportunity of coarse fishing to its devotees. Full details of all locations, clubs, riparian owners and conditions, are provided in *The Northern Anglers' Handbook* (Dalesman), available from information centres and newsagents. The Yorkshire Water Authority, whose rod licence must be carried by all anglers, offers a free *Customer's Guide* to all locations.

Canal cruising

Closely linked with the history and economy of the southern parts, the Leeds to Liverpool Canal can offer a different perspective to the Dales and adjacent area, or act as a base for excursions into the National Park. Traditional narrow boats are hired on a weekly basis from Pennine Cruisers, 19 Coach St, Skipton or IML, Bank Newton, Skipton, North Yorkshire.

It is not possible to detail all the activities open to the visitor. Those seeking a new and exciting experience may well be attracted by the hot air balloon flights operated from Grassington. Some may wish to watch the graceful soaring hang gliders concentrated around the scars above Hawes. Some will want to join with the Dalesfolk in their village galas and agricultural shows often featuring fell races and sheep dog trials; in the annual brass band contest at Hardraw or the sulky racing at Hawes; in the snooker, carpet bowls and badminton offered by village institutes; or in the cultural offerings of the Grassington, Settle and Richmond festivals of the arts.

The character and beauty of the Yorkshire Dales has been shaped over countless generations by the people who live in them and their stewardship of their inheritance. Increasing dependence on technological innovation has reduced demand for agricultural labour, setting in motion a process of depopulation often manifested by the closure of village schools and shops, and the decimation of bus and other essential services. Tourism is seen as one possible factor in reversing that process.

Partly for this reason, but principally because they want to share the heritage of which they are so justifiably proud, the people of the Dales offer you a warm welcome and generous hospitality.

Looking down on Littondale

The Pennine Way through the Dales

The 270 miles of the Pennine Way, Britain's first, and arguably finest Long Distance Footpath, hold a special fascination for all ramblers. The Pennine Way is the hillwalkers' Everest without the distance or the dangers, something to be tackled because 'it's there'. If you are young and strong and have three weeks to spare, a pack on your back and are prepared to pit yourself against the worst that the elements can throw at you across the wildest country in Britain, the Pennine Way can be yours.

But lesser mortals can also enjoy the Pennine Way on a less epic scale. You can, of course, confine yourself to a short length, finding pleasant pubs, youth hostels or guesthouses at which to stay. If you have a willing friend with a car you can be dropped off and collected at various points to enjoy the Pennine Way in day stages, and better still, if you are prepared to take just a little trouble with bus and rail timetables, you can complete a good deal of the Way, at least in its southern and central sections, by making use of public transport. The Ramblers' Association produces an excellent Bed and Breakfast Guide which includes many addresses on the Pennine Way, whilst the Pennine Way Council, a national body established to co-ordinate information about the footpath, produces an accommodation guide which also details local transport.

Contrasting scenery

If you are choosing a section to walk as an introduction to the Pennine Way, there is no doubt that the 60 miles or so within the Yorkshire Dales offer the finest range of scenery. This is the Pennine Way at its best, full of contrast, with moments of real drama, areas of heart-stirring beauty without any of the long, and occasionally dreary slogs across nondescript moorland to be endured in parts of the northern Peak District, or again in Durham and Northumberland.

Exactly where the Yorkshire Dales begin as you

The Pennine Way above Horton – a walk along the backbone of England.

follow the Way across the gritstone and acid moorland of the South Pennines and Brontë Country is open to speculation, but the charming valley of Lotherside, with its first hint of soft-grey limestone, and the subtle greens of more fertile pastures, has as good a claim as any.

A good starting point

For practical purposes the mill village of Cowling, with its twin hamlet of Ickornshaw, is a good starting point. On the main A6068 Colne-Keighley road, it has an hourly bus service between Keighley and Burnley. So it is quite simple to leave a car in Keighley to return on a choice of transport via Skipton.

From Ickornshaw, its name an evocative reminder of the oakwoods that once covered the Pennines (Ickorn = acorn) a mixture of lane and fieldpaths across soft pastures, across a little valley and a low hillock, bring you to Lothersdale.

The quiet valley that contains Lothersdale village will be the first real surprise and delight of this part of the Pennine Way. It is a mill village, and the mill has a mighty 45 foot waterwheel, now preserved as an important monument. The village post office welcomes walkers with tea, and there is a pleasant inn.

A climb to Pinhaw

The first real climb into the true Dales country now begins, at first a gentle ascent of a long green pasture, but soon a winding path across heather moorland to the craggy summit of Pinhaw Beacon. Pinhaw may be a mere 1273 feet high, but, if the weather is clear, the whole of the Yorkshire Dales unfolds before you – the magnificent limestone ridges above Malham, the peaks of Ingleborough and Pen-y-ghent and, over to the north-west the distant tops of the Langdale Pikes. Pinhaw was one of the chain of beacons which crossed northern England and was used in Tudor times to carry messages of major significance – such as the pending invasion by the Spanish Armada in 1588. Beamsley Beacon, across in Wharfedale is the next beacon in the chain.

Tracks and paths now descend to Thornton in Craven (hourly Ribble bus service to Skipton for Keighley) where the village shop supplies walkers with mugs of tea. Winding paths across farmland and low hillocks soon lead to the towpath of the 18th-century Leeds-Liverpool Canal and an extraordinary double arch bridge that still carries the thundering traffic of the A59. The Cross Keys Inn and the village shop supply refreshment.

Quiet, meandering paths which, in spite of waymarking, require careful map-reading (whoever described the Pennine Way as a 'pedestrian motorway' never walked the Way in this part of Craven) find their way across pasture, past little copses, across drumlins (low hills of glacial origin) into Gargrave.

A natural break

Gargrave makes a natural breaking point for the Pennine Way walker. The village is an old coaching town on the Leeds-Kendal road, now the A65, and has cafés, shops, pubs, an hourly bus service (Pennine Motors) into Skipton and a direct rail service from its little unstaffed station on the Leeds-Morecambe line to and from Keighley. After a 12 mile walk from Cowling, it's a natural end to a pleasant day to enjoy refreshment and await return transport from a greystone village whose little, unpretentious graveyard was the last resting place of a Chancellor of the Exchequer – the Rt. Hon. Ian Macleod.

The second stage

If Cowling to Gargrave makes a natural first stage of the Pennine Way in the Dales, the next stage might well be a leisurely seven mile stroll into Malham village. There are more of those lovely, low green hills to cross, the pale grey drystone walls and light, spongy pasture indicating the limestone bedrock of the soil. Nothing can compare with limestone country for the walker – dry underfoot, sweet scented in spring when wild flowers and herbs cover every bank, old barns and farmhouses that seem to have grown out of the very earth, and always as you walk north, the romantic turrets and crags of limestone on the far ridges.

You are soon following the infant River Aire, the river which, dark and sluggish, finds its way eventually through Leeds. Here it is bright, sparkling, following a shallow valley below Airton and Kirkby Malham, past an old mill or two where in less profligate times the energy of the river turned wheels of manufacture. It is the sign of these same times that the mills are now country cottages or flats for commuters or weekend visitors.

Historic Malham

Malham is an unpretentious little village in a magnificent setting, a great bowl of the hills which focuses on two great natural features – the massive Cove and the awe-inspiring Gordale Scar. If you arrive early in Malham, call in at the National Park Information Centre, close to where the Pennine Way enters the village, and learn something of the remarkable natural history of the area, where the effects of the faulting of the Great Scar Limestone has produced some of the finest examples of karst limestone scenery in the British Isles. Equally fascinating is the story of man's occupation of the area, from Bronze and Iron Age times (Iron Age fields can still be deciphered on the hillsides around the village, through monastic occupation to the modern hill farmer, coping with the pressure of the modern visitor invasion. If you have time before catching the late afternoon Pennine bus down the valley take the classic walk from the village past the Cove to Gordale (please do not climb the falls which already suffer severe problems of erosion) to Janet's Foss and back to the village.

Walkers pause on the limestone pavements above Malham Cove

On limestone pavements

The next stage from Malham might well be a long and strenuous one. It begins with an ascent of the side of the Cove, that magnificent natural ampitheatre of limestone which once carried a waterfall of Niagara-like proportions, to cross the limestone pavements of the summit (care required) – polished and eroded limestone whose clints (stones) and grikes (cracks) are a major feature of the Dales. The view from the pavement, down Malhamdale is quite ethereal, looking across to Pendle Hill in Lancashire.

A monastic track, Trougate, now takes the Pennine Way through craggy limestone pastures, evocatively named Prior Rakes (a sheep walk managed by the monks of Bolton Priory) to Malham Tarn, a beautiful, natural lake in a superb setting. Malham Tarn House at the edge of the lake, originally a shooting lodge of Lord Lister, was the country seat of Walter Morrison, Victorian philanthropist. The famous art critic and essayist John Ruskin was a frequent visitor here, as was Charles Kingsley, novelist, best remembered for *The Water Babies*, the didactic novel which owed much of its inspiration to Malham Tarn and the scenery of Malhamdale and nearby Littondale.

Field Studies Centre

The Pennine Way goes through the estate woodland, now a Nature Reserve, part of a scientific reserve of international importance. Tarn House is now a Field Studies Centre, a base for teaching and research of wide repute which offers a number of fascinating short and holiday courses, for the beginner as well as the expert, in various aspects of Dales natural and local history.

From the Tarn the Way swings northwards again, across more pasture, climbing close by Tennant Gill farm and the long, winding ascent of Fountains Fell. As its name implies, Fountains Fell was owned and managed, with its ring of outlying granges and farms, by the monks and lay brothers of Fountains Abbey, whose industry and expertise laid the foundations of the modern Yorkshire woollen industry, initially exporting wool via the Abbey to York and the Renaissance city states of Italy, later to develop the great West Riding manufacturing tradition.

Approaching Pen-y-ghent

If it is a dullish, steady climb up this great fellside, the summit cairns once reached afford superb views, most specially and dramatically across the Pennine Way's next major objective, Pen-y-ghent, which stands in majestic profile across the intervening valley. But tough, wild walking lies ahead, down the old miners' path to Dalehead, and the well used path up the shoulder of Pen-y-ghent, which soon becomes extremely steep.

By anyone's standards Pen-y-ghent is a real mountain. Though a mere 2273 feet, in form and ruggedness its mountain character is unmistakable, which anyone who struggles up the steep boulderfield to the flat summit plateau will appreciate. The view from the summit, in clear weather, is superb – across Ribblesdale, to Ingleborough and Whernside, the other two 'Three Peaks' to the head of Littondale, across to the Bowland hills of Lancashire. There is a sense of space and beauty about Pen-y-ghent, in good weather one of England's finest summits, its Celtic name signifying 'Hill of the Border' no doubt of the Celtic kingdom of Brigantia in pre-Roman times.

The ascent into Ribblesdale begins along a fine miner's track, but soon crosses one of the worst erosion problems of the Pennine Way, exacerbated by the Three Peaks Marathon walk, where the delicate peat surface has been damaged by the pressure of thousands of boots. Keep to the National Park boardwalks and causeways to help minimise the damage.

You soon pass Hunt Pot, an awesome natural fissure in the surface of the limestone, then descend Horton Scar Lane, a long stony track into Horton in Ribblesdale.

North from Horton

Though dominated by massive nearby quarries, Horton has many attractions for the walker, notably the excellent Pen-y-ghent Café in the village centre, which welcomes Pennine Way walkers, and the Crown Inn. Whaites' bus service will carry the weary walker back into Settle, with connecting bus service to Gargrave and Skipton for a parked car after what will have been a strenuous 15 mile day of fell and mountain walking.

From Horton northwards if you are using public transport you'll need to do a little research.

Signposts spur the weary walker on to Pen-y-ghent's distant summit

On certain weekends Dales Rail bus and train services link Horton Station with Hawes, whilst Ribble Motors have a summer weekend service between Settle, Horton and Hawes. The walking is easy enough, tracks and green ways on relatively easy gradients through fine countryside, 15 miles to Hawes.

This is a grand, wild landscape, its ruggedness relieved by beautiful gills where rowan and birch cling and in spring primroses flash their delicate beauty. You pass several small potholes, some with waterfalls and the occasional intrepid, wet-suited caver making his way down. From Ling Gill with its ancient bridge and Nature Reserve the Pennine Way climbs to the summit of Cam Fell along an ancient coach road where the Cam High Way, a Roman road, is followed to Kidhaw Gate. This is one of the great watersheds of England, with the source of the River Wharfe nearby on Cam Fell which eventually finds its way via the Humber into the North Sea and to the west, the source of the Ribble which emerges in the Irish Sea.

The Pennine Way strikes off the Roman Road along the side of Dodd Fell, grand views northwards now to Swarth Fell and the distinct and characteristic outline of Wild Boar Fell, reputedly where the last wild boar in England was shot, before descending to the village of Gayle and the little Wensleydale town of Hawes.

Hawes has great character, a busy market town (market day Tuesday) with shops, pubs, cafés, accommodation, the excellent Museum of Upper Dales Life and National Park Information Centre in the old station and weekend return bus to Skipton and Horton.

A spectacular waterfall

If Wensleydale is a dale to linger in, offering superb delights for the walker prepared to discover its secrets, the climb between the two valleys has much to offer.

It begins easily enough by fieldpath to Hardraw where a visit to Hardraw Force through the grounds of the Green Dragon Inn is not to be missed. This 96 foot high shimmering column of water is reputedly the highest above ground in England. Painted by Turner, it is in a natural rocky amphitheatre used every spring for a Brass

Top: Swaledale, one of the Way's finest views. Left: Lonely Tan Hill Inn north of Keld

Band Contest where bands throughout the north compete. The intrepid can actually stand behind the waterfall and enjoy the shimmering curtain of water, though expect some spray on your anorak.

From Hardraw begins the ascent of Great Shunner Fell, the gradient never steep. Initially the Way follows an old walled, stony lane, then crosses wild, boggy, peaty moor, churned up after rain. This is a remote and bleak summit, at 2340 feet higher than Pen-y-ghent but less dramatic, compensated, in good weather, by glorious views back to the Three Peaks, down both Wensleydale and, as you proceed northwards, into Swaledale.

Viking Villages

Swaledale is ample compensation for the ascent you have completed. You reach, by a long and stony track, the hamlet of Thwaite, its name as Viking as the early settlers of the valley. It was the birthplace of Richard and Cherry Kearton, pioneer wildlife photographers, and the Kearton Guesthouse has a justified national reputation for excellent food and accommodation – welcoming Pennine wayfarers.

Tom Stephenson, doyen of ramblers and originator of the Pennine Way, a man whose vision, imagination and dogged determination brought the Way into being, has confessed that there is no more beautiful part of the entire 270 mile route than that between Thwaite and Keld, as you ascend the side of Kisdon Hill to enjoy breathtakingly lovely views along Swaledale, across the village of Muker, clustered around its Elizabethan church. Little wonder that Swaledale has become enshrined, through the novels and films of the vet James Herriot as 'Herriot Country'; but its beauty is truly reserved for the walker, not the motorist or the coach tripper, as you will discover as you follow the Pennine Way up that hauntingly lovely hillside above the Swale past Kisdon and East Gill Force, to Keld, another Norse settlement and the last outpost of civilisation in this valley. You will have covered 13 miles from Hawes and on Saturdays between April and October there is a late afternoon bus to take you back to a parked car.

Lonely outstation

From Keld northwards there is no public transport to reach that lonely outstation of the Dales at Tan Hill, so as it is but six miles away, best to plan a circular return trip coming back by West Stonesdale, Robert's Seat and Raven's Seat. This is wild, empty countryside, some of the bleakest, loneliest and most fiercesome in England. Judge your arrival at Tan Hill Inn at opening time; apart from the moorland inn, with its own coal mine, there is no other human habitation.

Beyond Tan Hill there is a long wild tramp across even more rugged and desolate countryside until the delights of Teeside beyond Stainmoor Gap, stuff for the true Pennine Way devotee, but beyond the Yorkshire Dales.

If you are planning even a short walk on the Pennine Way in the Dales go well equipped – boots, rainwear, food, good maps, a compass. People have died of exposure on the tops. Leave word where you are going. Though waymarking is good, you must have large scale maps – at very least 1:50 000 *Landranger* series 103, 98, 92, preferably 1:25 000 *Outdoor Leisure Malham and Upper Wharfedale* and *The Three Peaks* for the sections from Gargrave to Hawes. Tom Stephenson's HMSO Guide is invaluable, as is Alfred Wainwright's classic *A Pennine Way Companion*.

USEFUL ADDRESSES:
Ramblers Association, *1/5 Wandsworth Road, London SW8 2LJ*
Pennine Way Council, *Hon. Sec, CDJ Sainty, 89 Radford Road, London SE13 6SB*

BUS SERVICES:
Service 25 (also Dales Rail) Keighley – Colne: *WYPTE, Metro House, West Parade, Wakefield, West Yorkshire*
Service 743 Colne – Thornton – Skipton; Burnley – Settle – Hawes: *Ribble Motor Services, Frenchwood Avenue, Preston, Lancs.*
Skipton – Gargrave – Malham; Settle – Gargrave – Skipton: *Pennine Motors, Gargrave, Skipton, North Yorkshire*
Horton – Settle: *DW Waites, 6 Halsteads Terrace, Settle, North Yorkshire*
Service 800 Keld – Hawes: *West Yorkshire Road Co, PO Box 24, East Parade, Harrogate*

Gazetteer

▲ Old Smithy, Redmire, Wensleydale

Each entry in this Gazetteer has the atlas
page number on which the place can be
found and its National Grid reference
included under the heading. An
explanation of how to use the National
Grid is given on page 74.

▲ The River Aire flows between old mills and flowery banks at Airton, on its way to Gargrave (and beyond to Leeds and the North Sea)

AIRTON
MAP REF: 95SD9059

This small township in Kirkby Malham parish has old houses spaced around a triangular green, some with dated doorheads. In the late 18th century cotton-spinning replaced linen-weaving, and the former riverside mill has now been converted into flats. The Pennine Way here follows one of its more gentle sections, as a pleasant riverside path heading north towards Malham.

APPLETREEWICK
MAP REF: 96SE0560

On the east side of Wharfedale two miles below Burnsall, and locally called 'Aptrick', the village prospered from 1300 when Bolton Priory acquired its manor with its extensive sheep ranges and valuable lead mines. Charters for markets and a fair were granted, and the fair remained important until the impact of the railways in the mid-19th century.

Stone houses line the steep, attractive main street between High Hall at the top and Low Hall at the bottom. The Tudor-style High Hall was restored by Sir William Craven, Appletreewick's own 'Dick Whittington', who became Sheriff and Lord Mayor of London at the beginning of the 17th century. He was born in a cottage almost opposite, one of a pair converted into St John's church, 1897–98, as a chapel-of-ease to Burnsall. Lower down is Monks' Hall, largely rebuilt in 1697 on the site of Bolton Priory's grange. This house has a projecting wing with an unusual façade, its door reached by an outside stair, and upper windows whose lintels are adorned with semi-circles, and pigeon-holes over the doorway and windows.

Two miles from Appletreewick, Parcevall Hall Gardens, covering 16 acres, display a wide variety of plants, shrubs and trees, many of which are rarely seen growing so far north.

ARKENGARTHDALE
MAP REF: NY9507 to SE0499

Arkengarthdale is Yorkshire's most northerly Pennine dale. Its place-names – Arkle Town, Langthwaite, Eskeleth, Whaw and Booze – speak of Norse settlement but its landscape is scarred with the remains of 18th- and 19th-century lead mining, touching the green valley with melancholy. Born on the lonely fells, the Arkle Beck's short but lively course takes it south-east from near Tan Hill to its meeting with the Swale at Grinton.

Travelling up the dale from Reeth, the inviting moorland road passes Arkle Town, the first hamlet, formerly with parish church, inn and workhouse. Now there are none of these, Langthwaite's huddle of grey stone houses form the focal point of the dale, with pub, shop, and unusual 'Waterloo' church of 1817, one of many then built with money provided by Parliament in an attempt to counteract atheism and free-thinking threatening the Established Church after the French Revolution.

Beyond Langthwaite is CB, the only place-name in England composed of initials. They commemorate Charles Bathurst, grandson of Dr John Bathurst, Oliver Cromwell's physician, who bought the Manor of Arkengarthdale in 1656 and developed the lead mines. The family connection continued until 1912. In a field by the road which turns off northwards to climb the Stang, heading for Barnard Castle, is the elegant, hexagonal Powder House of 1807, built to store gunpowder used in the mines. Near the CB Hotel a narrow road turns off to climb steeply past old spoil-heaps to cross the moors into Swaledale, negotiating on the way a water-splash in one moorland valley, and Surrender Bridge and the Hard Level Gill in another, in both of which broad areas of fine green turf offer suitable parking-places close to chuckling becks.

Back in Arkengarthdale the road continues to the head of the dale, passing the last hamlet, Whaw, and climbing steadily to the lonely Pennine heights by Tan Hill Inn, England's highest pub at 1,732ft, where one road branches off to Keld in Swaledale, and another heads westwards over the fells to Brough and Kirkby Stephen.

The annual show is an important event in many Dales villages, with sheep classes prominent ▼

32

ARNCLIFFE

MAP REF: 91SD9371

Of Littondale's four settlements Arncliffe is the largest, and the only one on the south side of the valley, approached most easily from the B6160 up Wharfedale by a minor road a mile beyond Kilnsey. Splendidly situated on a well-drained gravel delta above the flood-plain of the River Skirfare, Arncliffe's houses, cottages, farms and barns face inwards to a spacious green, outwards to green hillsides etched with long limestone scars. One barn on the north side of the green is a good example of the local style, with a porched entrance, and a datestone of 1677. Behind the village buildings are small crofts, almost one to each house; beyond them limestone walls climb the surrounding hills, separating higher fields, and the common pastures extend to the darker gritstone moors.

St Oswald's church lies close to the river north of the village, and the road up the dale crosses the river past Bridge End where Charles Kingsley was a visitor, to Old Cotes, a graceful house of 1650 whose gabled porch has a three-light window characteristic of late 17th-century houses in this area of the Dales. A narrow, winding road climbs steeply southwards from Arncliffe across the fells to Malham, an invitation to the heart of Craven.

ASKRIGG

MAP REF: 85SD9491

Most Dales villages sit comfortably at the foot of sheltering fells and Askrigg is no exception. Seen across Wensleydale from the main A684 five miles east of Hawes it is dominated by Ellerkin and Askrigg Common rising behind it. The minor road along the valley's northern side winds through the village, whose main street is bordered by stone houses in almost continuous rows, elegant three-storey ones presenting an almost urban appearance. Most are of 18th- and 19th-century date, arising from Askrigg's increasing prosperity through its clock-making, lead mining and textiles, and the Richmond–Lancaster turnpike which came through the village in 1751.

The street widens near the 15th-century parish church, and has a market-cross at its focal point and an iron bull-ring in the cobbles. Opposite is Cringley House, the 'Skeldale House' of the vet James Herriot in the BBC TV series *All Creatures Great and Small*. This is now an Abbeyfield Home – one of many ambitious community projects of the Askrigg Foundation, a charitable trust set up in 1971 with the initiative of Malcolm

▲ Scouring of hillsides by water – hushing – showed veins of lead ore

Stonestreet, then vicar of Askrigg. Low Mill, an outdoor pursuits centre for youngsters, with a recent extension for disabled people, and the craft shop are other successful projects of the foundation.

North of the church is a row of 17th-century houses, with a lane leading to an attractive short walk to the woods and waterfalls of Mill Gill and Whitfield Gill. Two miles east of Askrigg is Nappa Hall, a 15th-century fortified house (not open) whose towers can be seen from the road, while a public path passes close to it. West of the village the road continues up Wensleydale to Bainbridge and Hawes, while to the north exciting moorland roads cross the watershed to Swaledale.

JAMES HERRIOT COUNTRY

The world's most famous vet had his surgery in Darrowby, non-existent on any map of Yorkshire. It is a composite place, part imaginary but with strong flavours of Thirsk – where his practice still operates – Richmond, Leyburn and Middleham. To their west is the 'Herriot Country' of the Dales including all of Swaledale and Wensleydale with its tributary valleys of Raydale, Bishopdale, Walden and Coverdale. Herriot's practice did not take him over the watershed into Wharfedale or into the western Dales beyond Hawes; his country was the land of soaring fells, bare hillsides, stone walls, barns, farms and friendly villages of the northern Dales, the area selected by the BBC for location filming of their successful television series of Herriot's books, *All Creatures Great and Small*.

Askrigg became 'Darrowby', with Cringley House in the centre of the village, now an Abbeyfield Home, the 'Skeldale House' surgery-home of Siegfried Farnon, Tristan, and James and Helen Herriot. Dales farms, especially the more remote ones, provided the authentic setting for many delightful sequences, illustrating for millions of viewers throughout the world the unique, often austere, sometimes intimate, beauty of the Yorkshire Dales. For thousands of visitors now, 'Herriot Country' is as important as Brontë Country.

It is very real. The places and the people are real. You meet them in the villages, at the markets, on the farms. You can enjoy a drink at the Wheatsheaf Inn at Carperby where James and Helen spent their working honeymoon in a pre-war November; or in the Wensleydale Heifer at West Witton where they enjoyed so many meals; you can appreciate the quiet charms of Coverdale, where they spent happy holidays at West Scrafton; you can even drive through the same watersplash on the moor road between Swaledale and Arkengarthdale featured in the title sequence of the BBC series which introduced Herriot's Yorkshire to an enthralled audience.

Askrigg, the heart of Herriot Country ▼

AUSTWICK
MAP REF: 89SD7668

About five miles north-west of Settle and just off the busy A65, grey stone houses face small greens or border narrow lanes. The green hills and limestone country of Crummackdale, north of the village, are its chief attractions. The head of this quiet, remote valley is a gem of limestone scenery, with clean white scars, outcrops and pavements. Nearer to Austwick, and reached by easy tracks from Thwaite Lane or the Crummackdale lane, is Norber, a limestone hill on whose lower slopes are littered large numbers of dark, massive rocks. These are the famous Norber Boulders – in geological terms 'glacial erratics' – carried by a glacier during the late Ice Age from a source half a mile up the valley and dumped on this limestone plateau. Being harder than the rock beneath they have resisted erosion by rain and wind, while the rock beneath has been worn away leaving the huge boulders perched on small pedestals of white limestone.

AYSGARTH
MAP REF: 86SE0188

Aysgarth is in two parts. The village itself is on the main road to Wensleydale, the A684, and has no particular distinction. Over half a mile to the east, near Palmer Flatts, the youth hostel and the church, a short, steep road descends to the river, crosses by a narrow stone bridge, climbs the northern bank to the National Park Information Centre and car park, and eventually links up with the minor road along the north side of the valley. The main attraction is undoubtedly Aysgarth Force, where the River Ure, confined between

At Aysgarth the River Ure falls over limestone ledges ▼

wooded banks, falls over a series of broad, shallow terraces in a system extending over a mile. The Upper Falls, easily seen from the bridge and roadside, have the most beautiful setting; to view the Middle and Lower Falls – the most dramatic – it is necessary to follow public footpaths, well-signposted, through Freeholders' Wood. A trail leaflet identifies and explains the significance of various aspects of geology and woodland. Improvements to footpaths now make it possible for visitors in wheelchairs to appreciate the Middle Falls. The track through Freeholders' Wood is very muddy in wet weather when, of course, the falls are at their best.

Freeholders' Wood is now owned by the National Park Authority, but its freeholders, mainly people in Carperby, retain certain common rights, including that of gathering wood. In co-operation with them the National Park has started a 15-year programme of coppicing the hazel. This involves cutting trees just above ground level, when the 'stools' then throw up new shoots which will subsequently be large enough to cut in 7–15 years. Managed coppicing is rare in the north of England. One area of under one acre is to be coppiced each year, and a start has recently been made.

Below Aysgarth bridge, which was widened by John Carr in 1788, is Yore Mill. Built between 1784 and 1785 as a corn mill it had become ruinous by 1822, quickly repaired and used as a corn and worsted mill, but was up for sale by 1851 and destroyed by fire two years later. Rebuilt immediately to twice the original size it subsequently had a variety of uses, being a flour mill from 1912 to 1959. Since 1967 its roomy interior has housed the Coach and Carriage Museum. Above the mill St Andrew's church is largely a rebuilding of 1866, its 4½-acre churchyard indicating its earlier importance as the mother-church for the whole of upper Wensleydale. The former 81,000-acre parish of Aysgarth is now sub-divided. Inside the church, the exquisite wooden screen filling the south side of the chancel was brought to Aysgarth from Jervaulx Abbey at the Dissolution of the Monasteries. It was carved about 1506 by members of the famous Ripon school of carvers. At its western end is the delicately-carved Vicar's stall made from two bench-ends from Jervaulx.

BAINBRIDGE
MAP REF: 85SD9390

The Romans came to Bainbridge about AD80 and established a succession of forts on Brough Hill, a natural grassy hillock to the east of

the village, occupying the site almost continuously for over 300 years. It gives a fine view of Wensleydale and of Bainbridge village whose grey stone houses are set round the edge of a large rectangular green, gay with daffodils in spring, sheep-grazed in the summer. Stocks are a reminder of past punishment, and the custom of horn-blowing between Holy Rood (27 September) and Shrovetide in early spring dates from the Middle Ages when Bainbridge was on the edge of a hunting forest of Wensleydale. Unfortunately the custom is now only occasionally carried out.

Villagers bought the manorial rights of Bainbridge from the City of London in the late 17th century and its affairs are in the hands of its locally elected Lords Trustees who ensure, among other things, that the green is well maintained. Although the Rose and Crown overlooking the green is dated 1443 its present appearance suggests an early 19th-century building. Unusually, Bainbridge has no Anglican church, but does have a Chapel and a Friends' Meeting House. Low Mill, on the east side of the green, has recently been restored,

▲ The late 18th century bridge and corn mill at Bainbridge

WATERFALLS

Water there is in plenty in the Dales, and where rivers and becks flow over different rock strata, eroding them at different rates, waterfalls are formed. Each main valley has its falls, with Wensleydale having the greatest number and most variety, although upper Swaledale has a concentration of falls around Keld.

Aysgarth Force, in mid-Wensleydale, is the most famous, for size and scenic beauty, with the River Ure tumbling over a series of terraces spaced out for a mile between wooded banks. Further down the river Redmire Force is far less spectacular and little visited, but by West Burton village in lower Bishopdale Burton Falls make a charming scene above a narrow packhorse bridge. Above Askrigg, and reached by a footpath from near the church, Mill Gill and Whitfield Gill falls are the highest waterfalls in one of the finest gill woods in the Dales, with leaps of 60ft, bettered only by Hardraw Force, near Hawes, access to which is through a pub, the Green Dragon, at Hardraw.

Set in a natural amphitheatre, Hardraw Force throws a shimmering curtain of water into a deep pool, and the adventurous can walk behind the fall. Two miles beyond Hawes Cotter Force is easily approached by public footpath, and is a charming little fall.

Above Keld the River Swale falls over broad ledges at Wain Wath Force but narrows into a more forceful leap at Kisdon Force some distance below the village. Nearer the village, and by the Pennine Way, East Gill Falls take a lively beck over a series of cataracts into the Swale.

Waterfalls in Wharfedale take the river over limestone ledges in an attractive roadside setting two miles above Hubberholme, while near Grassington a much heavier flow gives some sound and fury to Linton Falls, crossed by a new footbridge. Near Malham, Janet's Foss is reached by an easy and pleasant walk, while Ingleton can claim in its famous 'glens' (charge made), a fine series of waterfalls linked by a popular footpath culminating at the spectacular Thornton Force.

Hardraw Force is a spectacular waterfall in a natural amphitheatre whose acoustics are so good that band concerts are held here ▼

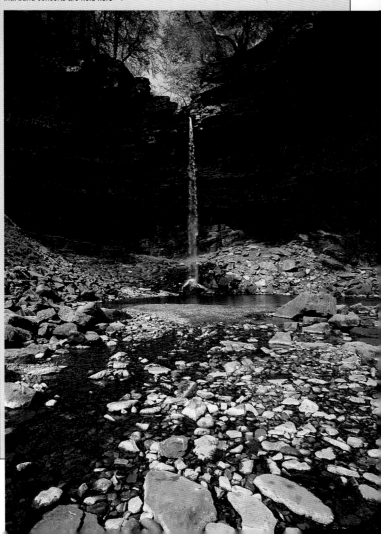

together with its fine water-wheel, and is occasionally open to visitors. England's shortest named river, the Bain, drains from Semer Water into a steep, two-mile course, entering Bainbridge over a fine cascade of waterfalls above the main road, and flowing down the eastern edge of the village into the River Ure.

BARBONDALE
MAP REF: 82SD6482 to 82SD6785

A minor road leaves Dentdale, west of Dent, and passes through the charming hamlet of Gawthrop before climbing steeply to cross a watershed and the National Park boundary into Barbondale. This wild, steep-sided short valley along the line of the Dent Fault marks the geological division between the limestones of Craven to the east and the Silurian rocks to the west. The unfenced road follows Barbon Beck to the woodlands of Barbon Park and the calm pastoral landscapes of the Lune valley above Kirkby Lonsdale.

▲ Stone walls pattern the valley and hillsides in lower Bishopdale

BISHOPDALE
MAP REF: 91SD9580 to 86SE0289

Three roads cross the watershed between Wensleydale and Wharfedale; from Hawes, Aysgarth and Middleham. The B6160 from near Aysgarth is the easiest road, threading its way up Bishopdale, the largest of Wensleydale's tributary valleys, a mile wide at its lower end and narrowing towards its head at Kidstones Pass, six miles away. Of the three villages broadly spaced at the foot of Bishopdale, West Burton, dispersed around its large rectangular green, is the most beautiful and the best-known; Thoralby is more compact, with a smaller green and some fine 17th-century farmhouses, while Newbiggin remains aloof, just off the B6160 near Street Head Inn, and is a small, linear village which ends at a farmyard.

In the Ice Age Bishopdale was filled with a glacial lake and the deposited silt has given the valley a fertile soil. During the Middle Ages, when Bishopdale formed part of the Honour of Middleham, it was preserved as a hunting chase for deer, but after Middleham's ownership ended early in the 17th century it became possible for tenant farmers eventually to acquire their own holdings, and as yeomen they began to rebuild their homes. As a result Bishopdale probably has some of the finest 17th-century farmhouses in the Yorkshire Dales, many of them distinguished with decorated dated door-heads. Good examples of these buildings are to be seen at Thoralby and Newbiggin, while nearer the head of the valley West New House (1635), and Smelter (1701), though off the road, have public footpaths passing close to them. Bishopdale's unusual orientation (NE–SW) has resulted in many of the farms on the east side of the valley being built to face south-east to catch the morning sun, and hence showing only their backs to the road. Smelter is one of these, but West New House opposite shows its fine 'long-house' frontage to perfection.

At West Burton Bishopdale divides, the main valley continuing south-west and the smaller valley of Walden entering from the south. Lanes leave West Burton to traverse each side of Walden but not joining at the valley head. There is no road out of the valley, which is dominated by the mountain of Buckden Pike.

BOLTON ABBEY
MAP REF: 97SE0753

Through long usage this Wharfedale village on the B6160 has become called Bolton Abbey although its famous ruins are those of a priory. Founded at Embsay in 1120 it moved to its present site in 1154, largely completed by 1220, with later additions. The west tower was started in 1520 but never finished, as a result of the Dissolution. However, after three years' recent work, the tower has windows glazed for the first time in 450 years and now has a roof with laminated timbers. The floor of the tower is to become a reception area for visitors. The nave of the priory church was allowed to remain in use as the parish church, whose 13th-century west front is a fine example of Early English architecture. The setting of the priory ruin is superb – riverside meadows, woodlands, moors and hills – so it is not surprising that it has inspired famous artists including Turner, Girtin and Landseer.

Romillys, Cliffords and Percys have been dominating influences in Wharfedale from Norman times to the 17th century, when a Clifford heiress married the first Earl of Burlington. In 1748 the last descendant of this family married a Duke of Devonshire, whose family still owns the Bolton Abbey estates. Developments by Burlington and the Devonshires have resulted in the beautiful parkland quality of this part of Wharfedale.

Bolton Hall to the west of the priory incorporates the 14th-century priory gatehouse into 19th-century extensions. Nearby, an archway over the road was an 18th-century aqueduct which carried water to a mill, and just off the road is a splendid tithe barn. Miles of public paths are an encouragement to explore Bolton Woods and the parkland, and a short way up the valley is the Strid, a narrow gorge where the Wharfe surges swiftly, 30ft deep, between rocky banks. A nature trail and accompanying leaflet explain various aspects of the wildlife. Car parking for Bolton Abbey, its parkland and for Strid Woods is available only at fee-paying car parks. There is no roadside parking.

The beautifully situated ruin of Barden Tower, three miles up Wharfedale from Bolton Abbey, was built in 1485 by Lord Henry Clifford, and restored by Lady Anne Clifford

▲ The beautiful 12th-century ruins of Bolton Abbey grace the wooded parklands of Wharfedale

RELIGIOUS SITES

For almost four centuries various monasteries extended their influence over the Yorkshire Dales and transformed huge areas of land. Cistercian monks, bringing with them great sheep-breeding skills, founded Fountains Abbey near Ripon in 1132, Jervaulx Abbey in Wensleydale in 1145. Augustinian canons settled at Bolton Priory in Wharfedale in 1155, while smaller foundations were established at Coverham in Coverdale in 1202 and at Easby near Richmond in 1152.

Of these Fountains Abbey is by far the most important, probably the outstanding Cistercian monastic ruin both for its church between 1658 and 1659, falling into disrepair in the early 19th century, but is still an impressive, three-storey tower-house. Chapel House across the yard, probably built in the 15th century as a chapel and priest's house, was later adapted to farmhouse use. Recent restoration has turned it into a small guesthouse and restaurant, while nearby a splendid barn has been converted into a bunkhouse barn (see page 38) providing simple, self-catering overnight accommodation.

BRIMHAM ROCKS
MAP REF: 77SE2164

Outside the National Park area but still very much part of the Yorkshire Dales, Brimham Rocks lie between the B6265 Ripon–Pateley Bridge road and the B6165 Harrogate–Pateley Bridge road. Almost 400 acres of moorland contain, in an area of about 50 acres, a unique piece of British scenery. Fretted, eroded pillars and blocks of dark millstone grit protrude from the bedrock to heights of 20ft or more. Worn by weather into fantastic shapes they have fascinated since the 18th century. Victorian tourists gave fanciful names to many – Sphinx,

Turtle, Dancing Bear, Idol, Anvil, Castle, Pulpit, Druid's Altar – and the grotesque shapes are enhanced by their setting among silver birches, bracken and heather. The National Trust now owns Brimham (car park charge) and has improved many footpaths among the rocks. A shop and information centre have been provided in Brimham House, a quarter of a mile from the car park. No vehicles are allowed in the area of the rocks themselves, so visitors need to be prepared to walk. Wheelchair access is straightforward, and all-weather paths have recently been completed.

BUCKDEN
MAP REF: 91SD9477

Nestling at the foot of Buckden Pike (2,302ft) in Upper Wharfedale, Buckden was settled in late Norman times in order to serve the hunting forest of Langstrothdale Chase. The road up Wharfedale divides here, the main one climbing over Kidstones Pass into Bishopdale and Wensleydale, the minor one continuing up Langstrothdale and over Fleet Moss to Hawes. A popular footpath follows the Roman road through Rakes Wood to Cray; other tracks lead over the hills to Littondale, up the ravine by Buckden Beck, or merely encourage more gentle walking through riverside meadows. Much of the valley and surrounding hills is now owned by the National Trust.

BURNSALL
MAP REF: 96SE0361

Wharfedale's landscape changes at Burnsall. Above the village are the distinctive limestone uplands, with

gleaming scars and hillsides patterned with white walls; below Burnsall the valley becomes more wooded, gritstone walls are dark lines in the landscape, and the moorland skylines more sombre. The B6160 coming up Wharfedale from Bolton Bridge enters Burnsall near a riverside car park (charge) and winds its way between mellow stone houses of 17th- and 18th-century date, many with mullioned windows. Near the top of the street is St Wilfrid's church, approached through a 17th-century tapsel gate – a lychgate with a revolving 'turnstile' entrance. The church was largely rebuilt during the reign of Henry VIII but shows some 14th-century work including a beautiful, sculptured alabaster panel showing the Adoration of the Magi. Evidence of a much older foundation is demonstrated by the crudely carved Norman font, fragments of Anglo-Danish crosses of the 9th or 10th centuries, and two hogback tombstones of the same date.

In the south aisle a tablet commemorates Sir William Craven who, in 1612 at his own expense, 'repaired and butified' the church, rebuilt Burnsall bridge and the grammar school just below the church, which he had founded in 1602. It continued as a grammar school until 1876 and is now used as a primary school. Its appearance is similar to that of a small manor house, with a two-storeyed gabled porch and mullioned windows with leaded lights.

Exploring the riverside paths to Appletreewick, Hebden and Grassington and field paths to Thorpe are the best ways to see the beautiful Wharfedale countryside.

▼ Burnsall in Wharfedale

and its claustral buildings which, in the 18th century became the focal climax to the landscaped parkland of Studley Royal. Fountains Abbey and Studley Royal (National Trust) are designated a World Heritage Site. At Jervaulx (privately owned; public admitted) the dormitory and chapter-house ruins are impressive, while Bolton Priory is not only hauntingly beautiful in its setting, but displays superb Early English architecture. Coverham shows two bays of its nave arcade, and fragments of masonry incorporated into later buildings, while Easby's pride is its refectory (Department of Environment).

Richmond's glory is the splendid 15th-century bell-tower of the former Franciscan friary, north of the Market Place, while above the river to the south there are fragments of a tiny priory. The road to Reeth, through lower Swaledale, passes the ruined tower of a very poor 13th-century Cistercian nunnery of Ellerton Priory, while beyond, on the opposite side of the river, very little survives of the church of a small Benedictine nunnery of Marrick Priory, and part of the building has been converted into use as a Diocesan outdoor pursuits centre.

CARPERBY
MAP REF: 86SE0089

The minor road along the north side of Wensleydale passes through Carperby, where houses straggle along each side of the single street which widens towards the western end into a green. In the centre, a high stepped cross, dated 1674, tells of the time when Carperby had a market (granted in 1305). In the 17th century the village became an important Wensleydale centre of Quakerism, and its biggest building today is the classically-styled Friends' Meeting House of 1864. This now houses the office and workshop of the Aysgarth Pottery.

The name of the Wheatsheaf Hotel suggests a corn-growing agriculture in the past, while, the inn itself was where James Herriot and his bride spent their honeymoon in the 1930s.

Between Carperby and Castle Bolton are excellent examples of lynchets – Saxon or medieval cultivation terraces in 'flights' of five or six, each terrace representing the deliberate levelling-out of part of a hillside to provide flat strips of land suitable for ploughing and the growing of corn. From near the middle of the village a lane leads northwards to the village stone quarry and the peat moors beyond, while to the south field paths lead to Freeholders' Wood by Aysgarth Falls, and to Redmire.

CASTLE BOLTON
MAP REF: 86SE0391

This is the name of the village, hill-perched on the north side of Wensleydale six miles west of Leyburn, half a mile north of the minor road up the valley. Unpretentious stone cottages line its single street along a green, with a water-trough at one end and the massive ruins of Bolton Castle at the other. Wensleydale's largest and most splendidly-sited building was erected by the first Lord Scrope, Chancellor of England, in 1379, more as a fortified manor house, with the needs of comfort predominating over those of defence. Designed with a huge, five-storey tower at each corner, four ranges of living quarters enclosing a courtyard, and turrets in the middle of each of the two longer sides, it took 18 years to complete. The original gatehouse entrance was in the east curtain wall but visitors now enter via an outside stairway on the west. The antiquary, Leland, writing in about 1546, asserted that it cost £12,000 to build, an enormous sum equivalent to about £1½ million or more today.

From July 1568 until January 1569 the unhappy Mary, Queen of Scots, was imprisoned at Bolton – in some degree of comfort, it must be said, with about 20 servants billeted in the village. She herself is thought to have occupied a large room in the south-west tower, with a fireplace, and steps leading to her bedroom. Bolton Castle was garrisoned for the Royalists during the Civil War, besieged by the Parliamentary forces in 1645 and eventually surrendered. Two years later it was partially dismantled and in 1761 the north-east tower, weakened a century earlier, fell during a great storm. The other three towers and the curtain walls survive almost to their original height. Now open to the public the castle's halls, chambers, battlements and dungeon, together with displays of armour, tapestries and tableaux, help to create an impression of everyday life at Bolton four

DALES BARNS

Apart from the farmhouse, often with its barn (or 'shippon') adjoining and under the same roof, the traditional Dales building is a detached stone barn in the fields. Most date back to the late 18th and early 19th century and were built to house small groups of cows or younger stock through the winter (mid-November to early May). Hay for their feed was cut from adjoining meadows and stored in the loft above; it was rationed out daily, and the cows milked at the barns. Manure was returned to the nearby field.

Changes have occurred. Current practices, often arising from farm amalgamation, a change from hay to silage, and the winter concentration of cattle in large centralised animal sheds, have made many field barns redundant. Some have become derelict and others, especially where they are situated near roads or villages and thus close to main services, have been converted into dwellings.

Encouraged by the Dales National Park Committee and with help from the Countryside Commission, a number of farmers have converted redundant barns to provide bunkhouse accommodation for individuals or small groups who pay £3–6 per person per night for basic, self-catering facilities. Most of the 17 existing bunkhouse barns are on or near the Pennine Way, Dales Way or Coast-to-Coast Walk and are particularly suitable for walkers using these routes. The National Park Office at Grassington provides a list of these barns, but bookings for them must be made through the farmers who operate them.

Conversion to bunkhouses only scratches the surface of barn conservation. Recognising the importance of field barns in the unique landscape of the Yorkshire Dales the National Park Committee has recently introduced a Barns and Walls Conservation Scheme whereby grants have been made to farmers to restore crumbling barns and walls. Initially concerning only Swaledale and Arkengarthdale (designated a conservation area and thus opening the door to funds for restoration), major structural repairs, including re-roofing, have been carried out, as well as the equally important and less costly 'stitch-in-time' work. It is hoped that the scheme will be extended to cover other appropriate areas of the National Park.

Stone barns are a particular feature of Dales landscapes ▶

▲ Trees by the beck at Clapham

centuries ago.

Opposite, and completely dwarfed by the castle, is St Oswald's church, part of which during each summer displays an interpretative exhibition of some aspect of Wensleydale's history or wildlife. There is a convenient car park (honesty box) adjoining, and from the eastern end of the village a moor road climbs over to Grinton in Swaledale.

CLAPHAM
MAP REF: 89SD7469

Now by-passed by the A65 between Settle and Ingleton as it skirts the southern flanks of Ingleborough, Clapham has three claims to fame: one scientific, one botanical and one literary. James Faraday was the village blacksmith and the father of Michael Faraday, pioneer of electrical science; Reginald Farrer travelled the world in search of plants, and from the Far East introduced many new species into Britain and Europe; and in April 1939 a monthly magazine, the *Yorkshire Dalesman*, was founded in Clapham. Now simply *The Dalesman* it is the most widely read and successful regional magazine in Britain. Its editorial office, and headquarters of the Dalesman Publishing Company with over 300 titles to its credit, is a stone building behind the houses on the west side of the village.

More wooded than most Dales villages Clapham is blessed with a beck flowing down the centre, dividing the two roads and houses which border them, and in its progress through Clapham it is crossed by four bridges. At the top of the village St James' church is, apart from its Perpendicular tower, a 19th-century rebuilding. Clapham is largely an estate-village of the Farrers who,

coming to the area in the early 18th century, added to their estates, rebuilt Ingleborough Hall early last century, planted Clapham Gill with thousands of trees – larch, pine, spruce and hardwoods – dammed the beck to create a lake, and transformed the top part of the village near the church in the 1830s. Roads were re-routed and short tunnels constructed which still lead under estate grounds as rights-of-way to Austwick and Selside. The Farrers explored and opened up Ingleborough Cave in 1837 and the family's dedication to natural history, culminating with Reginald Farrer's exploits during his short life (1881–1920) are commemorated in the Reginal Farrer Nature Trail, established in 1970. This is now incorporated into the Ingleborough Estate Trail of about four miles (there is a National Park trail leaflet). The National Park Centre and car park on the east side of the village are used by thousands of visitors each year, for many of whom Clapham is an excellent base from which to explore on foot the many varied aspects of the limestone landscape immediately north of the village.

CONISTONE
MAP REF: 96SD9867

A narrow, winding road along the eastern side of Wharfedale between Grassington and Kettlewell is joined at Conistone by a link across the river from Kilnsey. Loosely grouped round a small green and along the road to Grassington, farmhouses, barns and houses are built of local limestone, with rendered walls and dressings of sandstone. Its Anglian (8th-century) pattern of settlement and farming is easily recognised, with meadowland by the river, arable fields with strip lynchets along the lower slopes of the

hills, and common pastures above the limestone scars. Different stages of enclosure walls can also be identified, older ones uneven and curving, those of the late 18th-century straight on the ground because they were planned on paper. Conistone's farmhouses and barns are mainly of the late 17th century, some of the latter having been recently converted, with great care and taste, into private houses.

COVERDALE
MAP REF: 92SD9876 to 87SE1386

Within the National Park area, Coverdale is the most easterly of Wensleydale's feeder valleys on the south. From East Witton and Middleham on the A6108, and from Wensley and West Witton on the A684, narrow lanes converge on lower Coverdale from Coverham to Melmerby, then head south-westwards into the wilder upper reaches of the valley before climbing to 1,650ft and crossing into Wharfedale at Kettlewell, with a very steep descent at Park Rash.

Formerly part of the Honour of Middleham, Coverdale has the fragments of an abbey, a parish church, two chapels-of-ease, seven townships and many hamlets and farms. The few remains of Coverham Abbey are in private grounds, but a right-of-way along a lane through the old gatehouse does allow a close view, especially of the former Guest House, now incorporated into a later house. Coverham Bridge throws a high single arch over the wooded River Cover, and Coverham church nearby is over-restored.

On the south side of the valley from the bridge a narrow road leads past Caldbergh to West Scrafton, to join the main road beyond Carlton. This larger road comes up the north side with a branch to Melmerby. Carlton is Coverdale's principal village, with some good 17th-century houses. One building has a prominent inscription on the wall above the door indicating it was the home of Henry Constantine, a 19th-century local dialect poet. Beyond Carlton the valley is known as the High Dale, with Horsehouse three miles farther on, its community focus. The name is said to originate from the fact that it was a resting place for packhorses on their journey from Wharfedale to Middleham. From here it is almost six miles to the top of the watershed, the road passing through the hamlets of Braidley and Woodale into wilder scenery, and it is hard to realise that according to Ogilby's map of 1675 this route formed part of the important road from London to Richmond, via Skipton, Kettlewell and Middleham.

DENT AND DENTDALE
MAP REF: 83SD7784 to 82SD6491

It is as though a Cornish fishing-village has taken root amid the soaring fells of the Yorkshire Dales – although the village is now in Cumbria. There is no easy way to Dent. From the east the sensible approach is from the B6255 Hawes–Ingleton road near Newby Head. Soon a twisting descent takes you beneath the towering arches of Dent Head viaduct into the charming valley of the River Dee. At Lea Yeat this swings westwards into the pastoral landscape of Dentdale, with the better road along the north side of the valley, reaching Dent in four miles. An alternative eastern approach, not suitable for nervous motorists, leaves the A684 Hawes–Sedbergh road at Garsdale Head, climbs to 1,760ft before the long descent into Dent station (the highest main-line station in Britain at 1,150ft) and joins the valley road at Lea Yeat. From the west Sedbergh is the only gateway to lower Dentdale, while from Ingleton and Kirkby Lonsdale narrow moorland roads offer navigational challenges and scenic rewards.

A spacious car park on the west of the village enjoys a magnificent view and makes it easy to explore this fascinating village on foot. Narrow, winding streets are cobble-carpeted from wall to wall. Sturdy stone cottages sit snugly beneath low-pitched roofs of heavy, dark stone slabs. Colour-wash, mainly white, relieves the dark tones of stone quarried locally, and hides its poorer quality compared with that of the main dales. Chimneys, often perched on corbelled stacks, rise above rooftops, creating a close-viewed serrated skyline against distant green hills. Black paint outlines the shapes of windows, adding pattern to the intimacy of friendly streets.

The Sun Inn smiles across a corner to St Andrew's church whose long, low profile and dated clock look down protectively on a neat churchyard with good views up the dale. Inside, Jacobean box-pews in the south aisle and shiny brass memorials to the Sedgwick family are points of interest. Near the southern entrance to the churchyard, where three streets meet, is the main focus of the village; a rough-hewn block of pink Shap granite, perpetually spouting water. This is a memorial to Dent's most famous son, Adam Sedgwick, one of the greatest English geologists, and whose father was the vicar in the 18th century. Adam Sedgwick attended Dent Grammar School, a tiny building adjoining the north side of the churchyard.

First-floor spinning galleries were once a feature of houses in Dent and farms in the valley, used by women and girls of the households to spin yarn from the shorn fleeces of sheep. Dent itself gained a reputation in the 17th and 18th centuries for its thriving cottage industry of knitting, usually of simple garments like stockings, gloves, waistcoats and caps, carried out by all members of a family in order to supplement meagre incomes. Dent women continued to knit, commercially, until late last century, and Kendal remained the main market for the products, as it always had been. The Dales Way, a long-distance footpath between Ilkley and Windermere, passes through the whole length of Dentdale, often as an attractive riverside path.

▲ Wild flowers add natural beauty to the ruined walls of Jervaulx Abbey in lower Wensleydale

EAST WITTON
MAP REF: 87SE1485

The A6108 from Masham to Leyburn makes a sharp turn at East Witton, by-passing most of the village but allowing a tantalising glimpse of a long, sloping green flanked by unassuming stone cottages. A closer view shows a similarity between the houses, but no planned uniformity, although it is obviously an estate-village. The Earl of Ailesbury, whose family had acquired the former Jervaulx Abbey estate two centuries previously rebuilt most of East Witton in the early years of last century, the houses and gardens occupying precisely the same positions as they had done in 1627, according to an old estate map. Five small cottages on the green were removed, and a group of six at the top of the green reduced to two. To the east of the village the church was rebuilt in 1809 on a new site by the road, replacing the old church of St Martin whose site to the south-east is now embowered in trees.

East Witton lay at the edge of Jervaulx Abbey park and, with Coverdale to the west, was well-suited for a market, acquiring a charter in 1307, which eventually died out in the 18th century. Jervaulx Abbey, 1½ miles to the east, was one of Yorkshire's great Cistercian monasteries, founded in 1156 and owning large estates, particularly in upper Wensleydale. Today, the ruins are in private ownership, but open to the public (honesty box). There is a free car park opposite the entrance. Exquisitely situated in a parkland setting the ruins are famous less for their architecture than for the wild flowers that grow all over them in a calm, informal beauty unruled either by herbicides, geometric paths, or the need for manicured lawns.

A very narrow road continues westwards through East Witton to Coverham, passing Braithwaite Hall, a large mid-17th-century hall now owned by the National Trust but used as a working farmhouse. It has a stone-flagged hall, some fine 18th-century panelling and staircase, and has been tastefully furnished. It can be visited by prior arrangement with the tenants, Mr & Mrs D Duffus (Wensleydale 40287).

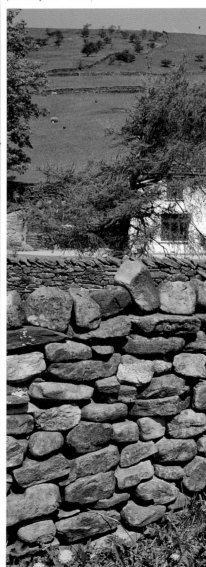

GARSDALE

MAP REF: 83SD7992 to
82SD6791

The only main road through the heart of the Dales, the A684, is a scenic east–west route linking the A1 near Bedale with the M6 near Kendal. It runs through Wensleydale from Leyburn to the valley-head, crosses the Pennine watershed at Garsdale Head, and continues through Garsdale to Sedbergh. Garsdale itself is a narrow, green valley extending about 10 miles westwards from Garsdale Head, between the steep flanks of Baugh Fell and Rise Hill, both now darkened with the conifers of private afforestation. Names of farms by the roadside or dotted along the lower slopes of the hills reflect Norse origins – Knudmaning, Dandra Garth, Thursgill and Raygill, birthplace in 1734 of John Dawson, who became an apothecary, a surgeon and eventually a famous mathematician. Becks tumble down steep courses from the fells, augmenting the quick, brown waters of the River Clough where trout glide in shady pools.

Whitewash brightens stone houses in The Street, the only community in Garsdale ▼

Garsdale is a valley of bridges, single-arched structures of stone built in the late 18th and early 19th centuries when the road was turnpiked, to link it with the farms and houses on the opposite side of the river. Some of Garsdale's houses are three-storeyed, more often only two, usually with narrower window-spans than elsewhere in the dales as a result of the poorer quality of local stone. White-washed fronts are commonplace and a few date panels survive.

Half way down the valley is its only community, consisting of a few houses, cottages, farms, church (rebuilt 1861), chapel (1841), post office, shop, school and garage. Collectively known as The Street, this is where the dale changes and widens, with more 'bottom' land becoming apparent. Stone walls of the upper dale give way to hedges, with a marked softening of the austerity. Three miles beyond The Street the road crosses an open stretch of Longstone Fell with panoramic views of the Howgill Fells, appreciated from a large roadside car park. Below, at Garsdale Foot, and spanned by Danny Bridge, the River Clough surges through a ravine of limestone and slate whose geological significance is explained in the National Park leaflet describing the two-mile long Sedgwick Geological Trail. To the west, the Clough joins the River Rawthey above Sedbergh.

DROVE ROADS

The droving trade, particularly of cattle from Scotland, flourished for almost 200 years from the end of the 17th century. Huge numbers of beasts, up to 200 at a time, in the charge of a drover helped by a boy and a couple of dogs, walked steadily southwards to the great English market of the Midlands and the south at 10–12 miles a day, along quiet, un-turnpiked roads, avoiding villages and cultivated land, crossing rivers and streams by fords. The drovers favoured wide open tracks and lanes, travelled rough and slept rough, occasionally enjoying a livelier night at a drovers' inn such as that at Gearstones, near Ribble Head. Small paddocks or wayside stances provided overnight grazing for the beasts.

Drovers' roads entered the Yorkshire Dales at Tan Hill, coming down Arkengarthdale, crossing Reeth Moor into Swaledale at Feetham, over to Askrigg, then by the Roman road over Cam Fell into Ribblesdale and Settle, or branching to Malham. An alternative route from Askrigg crossed the Stake Pass to Buckden in Wharfedale, Littondale and Malham. The highway above Mallerstang into Garsdale and across to Dentdale joined the Craven Way along Whernside's northern shoulder before descending to Chapel-le-Dale and linking with the Ribblesdale route. Some of these old ways are still lonely moorland tracks, others have become metalled roads so that it is hard to realise that around 1745 as many as 10,000 cattle were moving along the drove roads at any one time. Great Close on Malham Moor is still an enormous field north-east of the Tarn. In the 18th century its 732 acres were used for pasturing Scottish cattle, and in one summer 20,000 beasts grazed there.

By the mid-19th century the decreased demand for Scottish cattle and the development of the railways contributed to a steady decline in droving and the trade virtually ended by the turn of the century.

▲ Giggleswick church dates mainly from the 15th century

GAYLE
MAP REF: 84SD8789

Now forming part of the parish of Hawes in Wensleydale and almost linked to the market town, Gayle is the older community. The village lies at the foot of Sleddale, close-clustered on both sides of Duerley Beck whose course determined its setting and its shape. Beds of limestone form shelves over which the water flows and falls, fordable at the top of the village when the water is low, bridged lower down to carry the minor road to upper Wharfedale, which climbs out of Sleddale on to Fleet Moss, at 1,934ft the highest road in North Yorkshire.

Gayle's narrow alleys, some cobbled, have delightful names – Beckstones, Marridales, Hargill, Wynd, Gaits and Thundering Lane. Near the bridge Old Hall has an elaborately carved door-head dated 1695, but the village is predominantly one of cottages, although a few Georgian frontages add a touch of ostentation. Knitting survived as a cottage industry in Gayle more than anywhere else in Wensleydale. About 1784, a cotton mill was built by the beck, below the bridge, but soon changed to spinning wool for yarn, helping Gayle to become a centre for the knit hosiery trade, but the mill ceased about 1850, became a saw mill and is now a joiners' shop. Tall houses on the Beckstones were formerly combing-houses for the mill.

GIGGLESWICK
MAP REF: 94SD8063

The busy A65 crosses the River Ribble below Settle and now misses Giggleswick, leaving the village in relative peace to be explored leisurely on foot. In medieval times it was part of the extensive Percy properties in the north of England, and its church, dedicated to St Alkelda, dates from the 12th century, although most of the building is 15th-century work. Its long, low profile with no interior division between nave and chancel, is a characteristic style of Craven churches. Seventeenth-century woodwork includes pulpit, lectern, communion rails and almsbox, and a monument of 1841 commemorates Dr George Birkbeck, who was born in Settle and founded the Mechanics' Institutes which proliferated in industrial villages and towns from the 1820s.

Near the church are some fine late 17th-century houses of pale, local limestone, with drip-mouldings and mullioned windows. Colourwash is used to protect this rather porous building material. Friendly ducks enjoy the clear waters of Tems Beck, spanned by a single slate slab almost 12ft across. A beckside path leads to more attractive cottage-groups and the splendid 18th-century Beck House, now two houses, but all the while the scene is dominated by the landmark of the greened copper dome of the chapel of Giggleswick School. This famous northern boys' school, founded as a chantry school, was given a royal charter in 1553 and its present buildings west of the village show the Victorian Tudor preferences. The chapel, designed in 1897, was completed in 1901.

GRASSINGTON
MAP REF: 96SE0064

Some Dales' villages have the importance and character, if not the status, of towns, each serving as a metropolis for its own valley. Grassington fulfils this function for Wharfedale, yet retains its friendly village atmosphere. Historically important Wharfedale roads meet

GRASSINGTON VILLAGE TRAIL

Start at the bottom of Market Square, partially cobbled, at the heart of the village. Immediately on the west side is Church House, mainly 17th century (date-stone 1694) with Georgian windows above. On the opposite side is Grassington House, splendidly 1760, all symmetry and tall sash windows. Below this, on the east side is Pletts Fold, one of many small, compact groups representing 17th- and 18th-century infilling of crofts belonging to individual houses, built up as the village expanded. Beyond Grassington House and the Black Horse Inn, a former coaching inn, is the Upper Wharfedale Museum. Garrs Lane leaves the top of the square on the right, Main Street leading to Moor Road, on the left. The Congregational Church of 1812 is near the top of Garrs Lane, with Theatre Cottage, converted from a barn and used last century as a theatre. Beyond it to the left is Pletts Barn, now converted, but still showing its remarkable 17th-century character, with arched ventilation slits and pigeon-holes. Near the top of Main Street, which widens into a car park, is the Town Hall built in 1885 as the Mechanics' Institute, now the Devonshire Institute.

Chapel Street leads to the north-west, with more 'folds'. Seventeenth-century Town Head Farm at the end is its best building, contrasting with 19th-century miners' cottages on the way. Swinging left and left again, Garrs End Lane leads back to Main Street, passing Ranters' Fold and Chamber End Fold, where the end house facing the small square is a handsome 17th-century building with later window changes, but retaining its stepped, three-light window in the top storey – these small tripartite windows are a feature of houses in this part of Wharfedale. To explore fully every little alley and fold which give Grassington so much character and charm is a rewarding journey into the past and deserves at least an hour.

17th and 18th century houses in Grassington ▼

Until Tudor times St Andrew's Church, Grinton served all of Swaledale. Burials from the upper dale were brought along the Corpse Way

nearby: the B6265 Skipton–Pateley Bridge road and the B6160 from Ilkley up Wharfedale to Buckden and beyond. Additionally, the monastic route from Malham to Fountains Abbey passed through Grassington, so it is easy to appreciate why it developed.

Bronze and Iron Age settlement at Lea Green, north of the village, suggest an early favourable site, but the present Grassington is an Anglian settlement which, after the Conquest, passed through the manorial ownership.of Percys, Plumptons and Cliffords before descending to the Dukes of Devonshire. In 1282 it was granted a charter for a weekly market and an annual fair, and these continued until the 19th century. Change in land use from the early 17th century, when lead mining began to assume more importance, brought some prosperity, reflected in the building of many houses in the later part of that century.

But Grassington's heyday came during the late 18th and early 19th centuries, following new developments by the Dukes of Devonshire in lead mining on Grassington Moor, and the building of the turnpike roads. From 1790 the local textile industry expanded through taking over water-powered former corn mills, but when steam-power replaced water-power later last century the mills closed. At the same time lead mining declined, but the opening of the Yorkshire Dales Railway to Threshfield in 1901 brought new visitors, many of whom settled, perhaps finding work in Skipton or in the developing limestone quarries. Today Grassington is the main residential and tourist centre in upper Wharfedale, superbly situated, with good shops and other amenities, including car-parking, with the main one adjoining the offices of the Yorkshire Dales National Park.

Unusually, however, Grassington possesses no Anglican church, but has always shared the beautiful 12th century church at Linton on the opposite side of the river, with the three nearby townships of Linton, Threshfield and Hebden. Grassington has a lively arts festival in June and an artists' exhibition in August.

GREENHOW HILL
MAP REF: 97SE1164

Few villages occupy so bleak and exposed a situation as Greenhow Hill, on the B6265 between Grassington and Pateley Bridge. At 1,300ft it is one of Yorkshire's highest villages, developed solely as a lead mining community from the early 17th century. Lead ore had been mined at Greenhow in Roman times, but the industry did not reach its peak until the 18th and 19th centuries.

The scattered settlement, straggling along the road is loosely centred on the Miners' Arms, but its characteristic feature is the evidence of a dual economy. Numerous small, isolated cottages, each with its croft of land, and reached along narrow walled lanes, represent homes of former lead miners who kept oxen and horses for working in the mines. A few other livestock would also have been kept, so that the tiny income from a smallholding and croft might supplement money earned in the mine. Old levels, workings and ruined smelt-mills survive on the moors and in the little valleys to the north of the road. Stone-quarrying and the recovery of fluorspar from old spoil-heaps maintain an air of industrial activity about Greenhow Hill, but lead mining ceased by the end of the last century, and miners' cottages have become holiday homes.

Greenhow Hill is just outside the National Park, but within its boundary to the west are Stump Cross Caverns, a magnificent cave system discovered by lead miners in 1858. The main cave has been developed into an impressive show cave, floodlit to show visitors the splendid stalactite and stalagmite formations.

GRINTON
MAP REF: 86SE0498

Eleven miles west of Richmond the Swaledale road, the B6270, crosses the river at Grinton, leaving the gentler sylvan landscape of the lower dale for the wilder scenery and higher skylines to the west. Most of Grinton's grey stone houses and cottages straggle along the road to the south of the church or up the steep hill that climbs to the heather moors where two upland roads cross into Wensleydale. St Andrew's was the mother-church for the whole of upper Swaledale until Tudor times, and to its churchyard came burials from remote farms and hamlets over a dozen miles away. Fragments of the original Norman church survive but the long, low, broad building is largely 15th century.

A narrow road leads westwards to Harkerside, on the south side of Swaledale, passing some open common where junipers thrive, and there are fine views up the dale. On the moors above are prehistoric earthworks and the more numerous remains of large-scale lead mining activity of two centuries ago, including, by Cogden Gill, an early 19th-century smelt-mill. Grinton Lodge, on the moor-edge, is a 19th-century battlemented shooting lodge, used since the 1940s as a youth hostel.

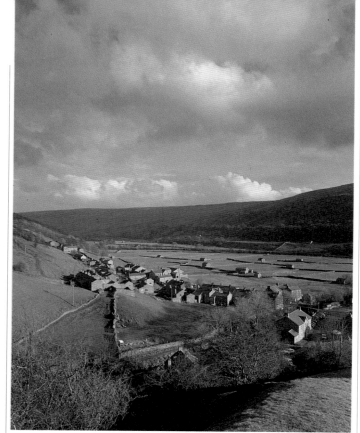

▲ Gunnerside was Swaledale's lead mining centre in past centuries. Former miners' cottages have now been converted to holiday homes

GUNNERSIDE
MAP REF: 85SD9598

Swaledale's austere, majestic, if sometimes melancholy, beauty seems to crowd in at Gunnerside. The road from Reeth, the B6270, along the north side of the valley, makes a sharp turn and crosses the Swale on a sloping bridge, to continue up the dale on the south side, a route taken only since about 1830. Before then it had kept to the north, along the route of the old Corpse Way. Norse settlers chose well this site by Gunnerside Beck, at the foot of sheltering hills to the north. Seen today from above the bridge, or better still from the road to Crackpot, Gunnerside is seen really to nestle, the meadows between it and the river are patterned with stone walls, dotted with hay-barns.

Gunnerside claims no architectural merit, no prettiness, no charm, yet it exudes the spirit of Swaledale. Stone from its huddled houses came from the fells above; dark, damp workings in the hills yielded the lead which enabled Gunnerside to prosper, and when the industry ended towards the close of last century the village declined. But between the wars and in more recent years it has become increasingly popular with visitors, and former lead miners' houses have been restored as holiday cottages.

Behind the village Gunnerside Gill cleaves its dramatic gorge between steep-sided fells, and nowhere in the Dales are the scars and ruins of lead mining seen in a setting of such wild beauty. A small car park by the former Miners' Institute is an encouragement to explore on foot (signposted and waymarked path) the east side of Gunnerside Gill. For almost four miles a good track can be followed to the lonely heart of the hills, by the beck or higher up, past spoil-heaps, ruined buildings, the small-arched entrance to old levels, and, most impressive of all, the savage hillside gashes caused by repeated 'hushings' in search of the valuable grey ore. A return can be made at a higher level along the eastern hillside, or by a good but tedious track on the west side of Gunnerside Gill.

HAWES
MAP REF: 84SD8789

Most market towns in the Yorkshire Dales are at the lower end of the valleys they serve. Hawes is different, being near the head of Wensleydale, 850ft above sea-level, with high fells to both north and south sweeping up 1,000ft beyond that. It is also a relative newcomer, receiving its market charter as recently as 1700, a recognition of the growth of its trade, mainly by packhorse traffic, in the previous century. No record exists of a settlement here until 1307 when, in the Forest of Wensleydale, it was Le Thouse, a pass through the hills.

Today, the A684 Sedbergh to Leyburn road passes through the small town (population 1,000) above the southern bank of the River Ure. Lesser roads lead north and south to the neighbouring valleys of Swaledale and Wharfedale, while the B6255 crosses into Ribblesdale on the route of the Richmond–Lancaster turnpike which came through Hawes in 1795. From the Moorcock Inn a few miles westwards, the B6259 branches northwards through Mallerstang to Kirkby Stephen and the Vale of Eden. Thus Hawes benefits from its position at the centre of good road communications as it also enjoyed a boom in the 1870s when the railway line came up the dale and was linked to the Settle–Carlisle line at Hawes Junction, later renamed Garsdale. The railway stimulated local trade and industry, particularly quarrying and dairying. Although many of the buildings of Hawes date from late Victorian times they are interspersed in the Market Place area and near the old bridge with houses of the 17th and 18th centuries.

Hawes is now the commercial and market centre of upper Wensleydale, with a good range of shops, hotels,

▼ Winter snow freckles the hills of Wensleydale above Hawes

guesthouses and holiday cottages, as well as camping and caravanning sites, and a popular youth hostel, reflecting its growing importance as a touring centre for visitors. Hawes' shops are small, independent family concerns offering good-quality goods, many of them made locally, and the good service at them and at the market stalls contributes to Hawes' reputation as a friendly market town.

Hawes Auction Mart is one of the most important livestock markets in the district; the Wensleydale Creameries in Gayle Lane (not open to visitors) is the 'home' of the famous Wensleydale Cheese. A large car park now occupies the former station yard, while in the old station and nearby goods warehouse is the remarkable Hartley/Ingilby collection of Dales bygones which forms the nucleus of the important Dales Countryside Museum. A National Park information centre and shop have been added, and it is intended to rehabilitate the station platforms, relay a short length of track, install and convert for display some rolling-stock and provide outdoor exhibits. At the Hawes Ropeworks near the entrance to Station Yard, skilled local craftsmen make ropes for agricultural, domestic and leisure purposes; visitors can see rope-making in progress. Various rope products and other craft goods are displayed for sale.

HORTON IN RIBBLESDALE
MAP REF: 90SD8072

The road from Settle to Hawes, the B6479, follows the River Ribble for 10 miles to its source near Ribble Head, where it joins the B6255 from Ingleton. Horton is about the mid-point, an ideal centre for exploring limestone landscapes, green hillsides, woods and caves of upper Ribblesdale. The village stretches for half a mile along the road from the corner by the church and the Golden Lion to the bridges by the New Inn, near which is a free car park, with toilets.

Horton's houses illustrate developments in the dale. Yeomen's farmhouses of the late 17th century are at the edge of the village, especially on its eastern side. Near the churchyard and the New Inn are later cottages, while Victorian terraces reflect the coming of the railway in the 1870s. More recent are the villas and quarrymen's houses built when the limestone quarries first scarred the slopes of Moughton, west of the railway, about 1890, and which have greatly expanded since the last war.

Eastwards, however, the view is serene and challenging, dominated by the proud, stepped profile of Pen-y-ghent (2,277ft), one of the famous 'Three Peaks' of upper Ribblesdale, its summit about three miles from the village, reached by the Pennine Way track along Horton Scar Lane, which passes close to Hull Pot and Hunt Pot on the way. Horton is one of the most popular stopping-places for Pennine Way walkers, whose subsequent route northwards follows old tracks along the eastern side of Ribblesdale to High Birkwith and Cam High Road. 'Three Peaks' challengers also like Horton as a starting and finishing point. These and other visitors will appreciate the calm benediction of St Oswald's church, grey-stoned, squat-towered, with Norman doorway and nave arcades. Lychgates to its churchyard are roofed with huge slabs of the ancient Horton slates.

THE HOWGILL FELLS
MAP REF: 82SD6798

When the Yorkshire Dales National Park was designated in 1954 the former county boundary between Yorkshire and Westmorland bisected the Howgill Fells in an east–west line. Bureaucratic tidiness incorporated the Yorkshire half within the National Park. This, together with the whole north-western sector of the National Park, is now in Cumbria but still lies within the Yorkshire Dales National Park. It is possible that the northern half of the Howgills will eventually be brought within the National Park.

The Howgills comprise about 40 square miles of green, rounded, lonely hills, smooth-sided, beautiful and uninterrupted by walls, hedges, or fences above the intakes. To their open, grassy uplands, reaching above 2,000ft, there is a tradition of open access, and walkers' rewards are of widespread, panoramic views, especially from the southern and western borders.

Valley roads clearly define the boundaries of the Howgills – A684 through Sedbergh on the south, M6 or A685 in the Lune gorge to the west, A685 along the upper Lune along the north and A683 in the Rawthey valley down the eastern side. Sedbergh, Tebay and Ravenstonedale are at the points of the Howgills' triangular plan. Walks on to the fells are most easily done from Sedbergh, Howgill Lane – a very narrow, scenic road from Sedbergh to Low Borrowbridge in the Lune gorge – and from Cautley in the Rawthey valley. But it is the long, remote valleys which penetrate from their northern flanks which reveal to the discerning explorer the secret, hidden places of these lovely hills.

▲ Sheep auction at Hawes Market

HAWES TOWN TRAIL

Start at the National Park car park near the small roundabout at the eastern end of the one-way system. Follow the one-way street into the town, passing first the Post Office, originally the grammar school of 1729. Cross Gayle Beck by Hawes Bridge. Upstream on the right is the former building of the Wensleydale Cheese Factory, downstream on the left the old building was formerly Hawes corn mill. Ahead, on the right of the narrow cobbled section of street, the White Hart was a coaching inn and staging-post, its busy years between 1795 and the railway era. Opposite and above is Hawes church, rebuilt in 1851, with many unmarked graves in the churchyard, an indication of poverty in late Victorian times.

Bealer Bank is a flagged causeway between the church and Gayle village, which can be followed, returning to Hawes by Gayle Lane, past the Creamery. Continuing from the White Hart into Market Place, the small butcher's shop by the Market Hall was the market toll-house, while the open space beyond the Market Hall, Penny Garth, was formerly used as part of the street auction of cattle and sheep. Beyond Gayle Lane was the 'hearse house', where the parish hearse was kept, but the 1643 date on the house below is misleading! Opposite is the working smithy, and the return journey along the north side of the Market Place passes Cocketts Hotel, formerly a Quaker rest house, with an interesting inscribed, dated lintel, 1668, above an adjoining doorway. Set back beyond it is Rose House, 1692, one of the best surviving 17th-century houses in the town. Barclays Bank building dates from 1889, re-fronted in 1920. North of the roundabout, by the Hardraw road, is the Quaker Burial Ground, given to the Friends in 1680.

HUBBERHOLME

MAP REF: 91SD9278

The road up Wharfedale, the B6160, divides at Buckden, the main route climbing over Kidstones Pass into Bishopdale and Wensleydale, leaving a minor, narrow road to continue into the wild beauty of upper Wharfedale. In a mile it passes the hamlet of Hubberholme whose church, dedicated to St Michael and All Angels, is now the parish church for the upper dale, but originated as a Forest chapel, and after the Dissolution of Monasteries was served by curates from Arncliffe in Littondale.

For thousands of visitors it is a place of pilgrimage, probably the best-loved of all Dales churches. Its superb riverside setting, against a backcloth of wooded hillside and distant bare fells, is a perfect frame for its broad, low profile and short, sturdy tower. The interior is memorable, with unplastered walls of rough local stone contributing to a remarkably medieval atmosphere, enhanced by the rare survival of an exquisite rood-loft of 1558, one of only two in Yorkshire. Carved in oak, painted red, black and gold, it is contemporary with much of the building including the windows and the tower. A modern window in the south aisle is a visual story of the parish, although it does not illustrate the time when the river flooded into

the church, and as its level receded fish were seen swimming in the nave. The church was sympathetically repaired in 1863, when the walls were stripped, and again in 1955–56. Almost all the woodwork is modern oak, made by Robert Thompson of Kilburn in 1934 and his signature, a tiny church mouse, can be identified on many of the pieces, usually hidden away in inconspicuous places.

The George Inn by the roadside was originally the vicarage, but remained church property even as an inn until 1965. Here, on each New Year's Day, is the ceremony of letting the 'Poor Pasture', a custom almost 1,000 years old, when farmers bid for the tenancy of a 16-acre field behind the inn which had been left in trust for the poor of the parish. The vicar used to perform the auction, but this is now done by a local auctioneer. Proceeds from it go to help old people in the parish. Between the inn and the church Hubberholme bridge was on an old and important route between Lancaster and Newcastle, noted as being in decay in 1639, ruined in 1709 and rebuilt in 1734.

INGLETON

MAP REF: 88SD6973

When the railway line came from Settle in 1849, and the dominating viaduct helped to extend it to Sedbergh ten years later, Victorian

▲ George Fox preached Quakerism

EARLY VISITORS TO THE DALES

The Dales have attracted visitors for over 250 years, although the earliest written accounts of visits go back to Tudor times, with John Leland about 1546 and the historian Camden in 1582. In the 17th century the northern Dales played an important part in the founding of Quakerism, and George Fox's preaching travels through the area are recorded in his Journal of 1652.

Celia Fiennes rode side-saddle through England in the 1690s, including Richmond in her itinerary, and finding it a 'sad shatter'd town much to Decay', while in 1724 Defoe's travels brought him to Skipton and Settle from where he saw to the north-west 'high mountains which had a terrible aspect . . . especially Penigent'. However, he did reach Burnsall and Richmond. Fifty

train-borne travellers began to put Ingleton on the tourist map. Today, the A65 following the route of the Keighley–Kendal turnpike of 1753, brings the motorist, although the main road now just by-passes the village. Lancaster is only 18 miles away by the A687, with Hawes the same distance to the north-east along the B6255. Good car-parking facilities near the community centre encourage a stay and some exploration.

Village streets are narrow and winding, centred on a tiny market place. Nearby the late Victorian church has one of the finest Norman fonts in Yorkshire. Bell Horse Gate descends steeply to the river whose water once worked mills, but these are now derelict, although their mill-worker's cottages form neat terraces almost in the shadow of the viaduct. Wool- and cotton-spinning were important local industries in the 18th and 19th centuries.

As long ago as 1884 a group of residents, recognising tourist potential in the local scenery, formed the Ingleton Improvement Society, and over the next thirty years created miles of paths, built steps and bridges along the increasingly popular walks up the valleys of the Doe and Twiss,

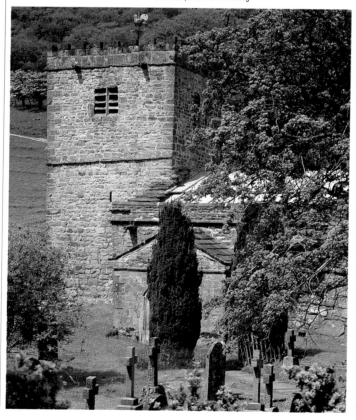

▼ Hubberholme church in Wharfedale has a tranquil riverside setting

▲ Kisdon Force on the Swale below Keld

years later John Wesley's *Journals* refer to successful meetings at Redmire, Wensley and Richmond, and six years on, at Grassington and Pateley Bridge.

Tourists, an early 19th-century word meaning people with sufficient wealth and leisure to travel primarily for pleasure, began to penetrate the Dales from about 1750 onwards, encouraged by improved roads. Bishop Pococke in 1751 was impressed with Wensleydale, in 1773 Thomas Pennant, *en route* to Scotland, found good hospitality in Settle, while 20 years later, the Hon. John Byng (later Lord Torrington) tended to find more to criticise than to praise, being distinctly upset by the new noisy cotton mill at Aysgarth Force. Thomas Gray was horrified at Gordale Scar's frowning crags in 1769, and in October 1802 Wordsworth and his new bride Mary, with sister Dorothy naturally present, travelled up Wensleydale on their honeymoon journey from Brompton, near Scarborough. They changed horses at Aysgarth, walked to the falls and stayed overnight at Hawes before continuing to Grasmere. Dorothy's *Journal* records the favourable impressions they all felt.

which, probably because the word sounds more romantic, were called glens. The 'Falls Walk' (charge) is today Ingleton's best-known attraction, with a small car park near the entrance. The Ingleton Waterfalls Trail is a five-mile walk (National Park leaflet available) following a well-defined footpath past waterfalls through varied woodlands and with fascinating geological features. On the Hawes road, a mile outside the village, White Scar Caves are another of Ingleton's special attractions, and are open daily.

Ingleborough (2,372ft) is the best-known, if not quite the highest, of Yorkshire's Three Peaks, its

▼ Catrake Falls near Keld

limestone-stepped bulk sheltering Ingleton on the north-east, a familiar and perpetual challenge. The ascent from Ingleton via Fell Lane and Crina Bottom is relatively easy, though rather tedious, with a steep climax to the summit plateau, once the site of a huge Iron Age fort.

Limestone quarrying has created unsightly scars above the village, but vanished now are the remains of Ingleton's coal mine south of the village. Although mining is but a memory the brick-built miners' houses of 1913–14 form an interesting 'new village' on Ingleton's eastern edge.

KELD
MAP REF: 79NY8901

Green hills enfold this tiny grey stone village at the head of Swaledale, 22 miles from Richmond by one of England's most scenic roads. The final switchback stretch to Keld is above a dry valley, the river's course having taken it round the eastern side of Kisdon's isolated hill. Cottages cluster close around a tiny square above the river, and one road ends there, with space for only a handful of cars. Two chapels, the school and the gaunt youth hostel at Keld Green, are the biggest buildings in this remote place.

The riverside scenery is superb, with the Swale sweeping into a wooded limestone gorge below the village, and crossed by a footbridge carrying the Pennine Way *en route* for the Tan Hill Inn four moorland miles away. An easy walk above the north side of the wooded gorge leads to Crackpot Hall (a ruined part; see Walk 1) and the dramatic ravine of Swinnergill. The Pennine Way enters the village by a high level route round Kisdon's eastern and northern shoulder. The much older Corpse Way crosses its windy plateau.

Above Keld, a lonely road heads westwards into the wilderness landscape of upper Swaledale and crosses to Kirkby Stephen. A mile along it a branch heads northwards, over Park Bridge, up a double-hairpin hill to West Stonesdale and Tan Hill Inn. All around is the austere grandeur of high Pennine fells, a landscape of wide horizons and splendid solitude.

KETTLEWELL
MAP REF: 92SD9772

In the 12th century, part of Kettlewell's manor was granted to the canons of Coverham Abbey across the hills to the north-east. Fountains Abbey and Bolton Priory also had estates here, so it was natural that a market was established in the 13th century, and the village became a thriving community. Textiles, and in the late 18th and early 19th centuries lead mining, revitalised village prosperity and Kettlewell's appearance today derives much from the past 200 years. The remains of the smelting mill, used from 1700 to 1886, can be seen near the confluence of Cam and Dowber Becks half a mile above the village.

The B6160, coming up Wharfedale from Threshfield, crosses the Wharfe into Kettlewell by a handsome stone bridge, and there is a good riverside car park immediately beyond this. Three inns – the Racehorses, the Blue Bell and the King's Head – testify to Kettlewell's popularity with visitors, and in addition there are numerous guesthouses and holiday cottages.

The main road touches only the southern edge of the village, and a stroll through its quiet lanes and turnings reveals a number of 17th- and 18th-century houses, including the vicarage. The church, however, is late Victorian. Apart from its beautiful setting Kettlewell's main appeal is as a base from which to explore the surrounding landscapes, along inviting riverside paths above and below the bridge, by steeper, rougher tracks up Dowber Gill as an approach to Great Whernside (2,308ft), to Starbotton by woodland paths or the exciting green lane of Top Mere Road, or, for the energetic, a climb over the tops to Arncliffe or Hawkswick in Littondale. The minor road to Conistone down Wharfedale's eastern side passes Scargill House, a Church of England conference and holiday centre with a church built in Scandinavian style. Coniferous plantations contrast with the paler greens of deciduous woodland and gleaming limestone scars etch the hillsides while valley fields display the planned geometry of late 18th-century enclosure, punctuated with stone barns.

▲ Kilnsey Crag overlooks the trout-fishing lake at Kilnsey Park in Wharfedale, with a Fish Farm and Riverlife Museum

KILNSEY
MAP REF: 96SD9767

Wharfedale's outstanding landscape feature is Kilnsey Crag, a gigantic thrust of the Great Scar Limestone towering 170ft above the B6160 four miles above Grassington. A remarkable 40ft overhang at the top has presented rock-climbers with one of their stiffest challenges. Earthbound mortals merely gaze in awe. During the later stages of the Ice Age the Wharfedale glacier scoured back the recessed base of the cliff, where springs gush out and form a roadside beck.

Kilnsey itself is a handful of houses and the Tennant Arms Hotel. Behind, by the road which marks the beginning of Mastiles Lane, is Kilnsey Old Hall, built in 1648 on the site of a busy grange of Fountains Abbey. The hall, now used as a farm store, retains its outside stone stair and by the courtyard entrance part of the 15th-century gatehouse of the grange survives. Mastiles Lane was a monastic track, now a green lane, leading to monastic estates on Malham Moor and beyond the Ribble to the Lake District.

Nearby, Kilnsey Park has been developed as a visitor centre orientated towards freshwater fish. There are specially designed trout-fishing lakes and a trout-feeding pond. In the farm shop fresh trout, smoked trout, pheasants, ducks and rabbits can be bought, as well as cold-water tropical fish. A 'Riverlife Museum' displays in a well-designed series of aquariums, a fine variety of British freshwater fish, and upstairs visual exhibits and audio-visual presentations illustrate many aspects of wildlife in the Dales.

Along more traditional lines Kilnsey Show, first held in 1897, is one of Wharfedale's most popular annual events, taking place on August Bank Holiday Tuesday. Livestock displays, sheepdog trials, rural crafts, flat races, galloping and horse-trotting, and the Crag Race, provide a series of exciting, competitive events.

LANGCLIFFE
MAP REF: 94SD8265

From Settle the B6479 road up Ribblesdale misses most of Langcliffe, which as a result enjoys a seclusion unusual among Dales villages. Informal rows of stone cottages keep their distance round a spacious green, most colourful in late October with a golden canopy of beeches. The village once belonged to Sawley Abbey in lower Ribblesdale, but in more recent times depended on its cotton mill. Although a few houses have 17th-century date-stones most suggest by their appearance that Langcliffe was a no-nonsense industrial community from the late 18th century.

A narrow road climbs steeply north-eastwards and crosses the uplands to Malham about seven miles away. Near the crest of the hill a good track leads to Victoria Cave, where discoveries of bones, flints and tools indicate cave occupation to 9000BC. Further south are the fine limestone cliffs of Attermire Scar.

LANGSTROTHDALE
MAP REF: 90SD8780 to 91SD9278

Above Buckden the upper valley of the Wharfe is known as Langstrothdale. Founded in Norman times Langstrothdale Chase was formerly a hunting preserve for deer and game, having its own forest law, courts, privileges and punishments. Settled in Norse times a thousand years ago by people coming from the west and north, its Norse sheep farms

The small Bronze Age stone circle at Yockenthwaite, Langstrothdale, indicates that early settlers found the area quite favourable ▼

became lodges in the forest, and these survive today as the hamlet-settlements in the valley – Cray, Hubberholme, Raisgill, Yocken-thwaite, Deepdale, Beckermonds and Oughtershaw.

Natural woodland diminishes beyond Yockenthwaite, the valley narrows and becomes wilder. The minor road from Buckden is unfenced here, with sheep-cropped sward on both sides for a while, and the river always close, following a course which takes it over limestone beds and ledges, where it forms weirs and small brown pools. Above Yockenthwaite, hidden behind a wall in a field across the river, is one of the few Bronze Age stone circles in the Dales, with 20 stones forming a rough circle 25ft across.

The road crosses the river at Deepdale by an iron bridge of 1907 (now itself being rebuilt) which replaced a stone packhorse structure. At Beckermonds the road divides, its northern arm climbing first to Oughtershaw at 1,200ft, and then to the watershed on Fleet Moss, 1,934ft, the highest road in North Yorkshire, before descending to Wensleydale at Hawes. From Beckermonds the other fork continues westwards through new private afforestation to High Greenfield, where the metalled surface ends. Greenfield was a Fountains Abbey grange so this route probably originated in medieval times. It subsequently formed part of an important packhorse way between Lancaster and Richmond; as a walkers' route today it crosses to Horton in Ribblesdale, joining the Pennine Way on Birkwith Moor.

LEYBURN
MAP REF: 87SE1190

On the important A684 trans-Pennine route between Northallerton and Kendal, which threads much of

DATE PANELS

'The great rebuilding', as it is often referred to, of houses in England occurred later in the Yorkshire Dales than in most other areas of the country. Apart from the more obvious fortified houses only Friars Head at Winterburn, and possibly West End House in Askrigg, are known to predate 1600. A few Dales farmhouses were built in Jacobean times, but rebuilding accelerated from the 1630s, peaked towards the end of the century, continued apace until about 1730, when it slowed down. One aspect of this rebuilding is the decorative treatment of door-heads, not only with elaborately carved lintels but with date panels often incorporated into the design.

The date panel at Cocketts Hotel, Hawes, formerly a Quaker Rest House ▼

Dates on them need to be treated with caution. They may accurately represent the date of a building or be the date when it was occupied as a marriage-house; they may date an alteration, an addition or an inheritance. They may not even refer to the building they adorn but have simply been taken from another structure altogether! Almost invariably, however, they are decorative and distinctive. Where only two initials are given they are probably those of the man who built the house. If three initials occur that of the surname usually dominates and is central, the others being the initials of the Christian names of husband and wife. Four initials are uncommon, but would probably represent Christian and surname initials of the pair before marriage.

The most decorative door-heads occur in the Craven area – Wharfedale, Littondale, Ribblesdale – with good examples at Settle. Particularly outstanding is the whole door case at Ingman Lodge, near Selside, whose unusual design incorporates an elegant hood, carved capitals and stone halberds, as well as the date panel.

Wensleydale, Leyburn has developed as the main market, commercial and trading centre for the dale. Yet is is a comparative newcomer, having received its charter only in 1684 when it was a village centred on Grove Square. Many of the buildings which front the large Market Place date from the early years of last century, but the Regency-style Market Hall was not completed until 1856, the same year as the railway arrived from Northallerton and Bedale. Although a single line passes through the town today this merely serves the quarries above Redmire and there is no passenger traffic.

Leyburn's present appearance is that of a prosperous, late-Georgian market town, although shop frontages have largely become anonymously modern. Some 18th-century houses survive, mainly around Grove Square, but the Bolton Arms, at the top of the Market Place, and Leyburn Hall, almost completely hidden behind it, are the best buildings. Unusually, until 1836 Leyburn had no Anglican church.

Townscape becomes landscape very suddenly on Leyburn's western edge. From the top of the Market Place, Shawl Terrace leads to an open, grassy terrace on a shelf of limestone. This is the strangely named Leyburn

▲ Leyburn has a lively street and livestock market every Friday

Shawl, from which a glorious prospect of Wensleydale is revealed, generously wooded in the near view, with the gently stepped profile of hills leading the eye into the distance.

With good roads leading northwards to Richmond, south to Middleham, Masham and Ripon, Leyburn is a conveniently placed tourist centre for lower Wensleydale and its hotels, holiday cottages and nearby caravan parks cater for an increasing number of visitors.

▲ The packhorse bridge in the centre of the village of Linton

LINTON

MAP REF: 96SD9962

Situated just off the B6160 on the south side of Wharfedale opposite Grassington, Linton is by any standards one of the outstanding villages in the Yorkshire Dales. Scenically, architecturally, and in terms of its later industrial development, it is full of interest. Sited on well-drained moraine gravels it was attractive to Anglian settlers and the village pattern originates from those times, with groups of houses informally set around a large irregular green. Linton Beck flows down the middle of the village, crossed by a clapper bridge, a packhorse bridge, a modern road bridge, stepping-stones and fords, and, near the river, Little Emily's Bridge.

Grey stone houses round the green, mainly of 17th- and 18th-century dates, display an unusual dignity, partly explained by the dominating presence of Fountaine Hospital, founded and endowed in 1721 by Richard Fountaine, 'for six poor men or women'. He was timber merchant for Sir John Vanbrugh and it is possible that the great architect may have designed this remarkable structure, far grander than any other building in Wharfedale. Fountaine Hospital introduced the classical style of building not only to Wharfedale but to the Dales area in general, its symmetry and classical motifs were subsequently copied and adapted for Dales houses throughout the rest of the 18th-century, usually on a much smaller scale.

At the other end of the green, by the main road, Old Hall shows at its western end typical late 17th-century features, but at the eastern end is a three-storey enlargement of early Georgian times, with a handsome porch and tall sash windows. Nearby is White Abbey (never monastic), a typical 17th-century yeoman's house. 'Beckside', in a fold off the east side of the green, is similarly long and low,

with a decorated lintel and datestone of 1642.

Beyond the main road, and half a mile from the village, Linton Church serves the community of Grassington, Threshfield, Hebden and Linton, each having footpaths leading to it. The late 12th-century building, with its squat bell-turret, shows Norman features, but was largely rebuilt and extended during the 15th century.

Until 1866 Linton had two rectors, the result of there having been two Lords of the Manor, each with the right of advowson.

On the road to the church is a small car park, opposite a terrace of mill cottages dating from 1850 which were built for workers in the nearby Linton Mill (demolished in the 1980s and recently replaced by a development of small stone cottages). Linton Mill was built on the site of an earlier one used for spinning worsted cloth and, after 1840, cotton, utilising water-power from the River Wharfe above Linton Falls where a new footbridge carries the church path from Grassington across the river.

LITTONDALE

MAP REF: 90SD8776 to 91SD9769

Charles Kingsley called it Vendale, Wordsworth named it Amerdale and ITV chose it for *Emmerdale*. However, the Ordnance Survey correctly identifies it as Littondale, and the river draining it is the Skirfare. Two minor roads enter the valley from

THE DALES AND THE ARTIST

Perhaps because Art rarely flourishes in an area where climate and environment create harsh living conditions it is not until the relatively easier times of this century that the Dales can claim strong residential associations with artists. However, artists of national repute have found great inspiration in Dales landscapes, led by Girtin. In 1796 he made a lengthy tour of the North and did much sketching around Bolton Abbey, Malham and Richmond, as well as at Greta Bridge and Barnard Castle in Teesdale. Dales scenery between the Wharfe and the Tees features in over thirty water-colours based on these sketches. His work may have influenced Cotman and De Wint, both of whom visited the area, and Constable. It is more than likely that Turner felt encouraged to see the Dales for himself and travelled to Yorkshire to visit the places which Girtin had painted.

Entering by way of Knaresborough and Ripon he went on to Richmond and Teesdale, continued further north to Northumberland, returning by way of the Lake District and Lancaster to Settle, Skipton and Bolton Abbey. Three Yorkshire

scenes were exhibited the next year, 1798, in the Royal Academy. Commissioned work, to illustrate Whitaker's *History of Craven* and *History of Richmondshire* brought Turner to Yorkshire again on an extended tour, and he was also asked to paint scenes in Wharfedale and the Craven area for Walter Fawkes of Farnley, near Otley. From 1808 to 1825 Turner spent part of each summer in the Dales, and produced many paintings and drawings of Wensleydale, Swaledale and Teesdale, Bolton, Barden, Gordale and Ribblesdale, including the caves.

In recent times the artistic tradition has been carried on by painters like Fred Lawson, who came as a young man to Castle Bolton in 1911 and stayed until his death in 1968, and Marie Hartley, E. Charles Simpson, Constance Pearson, Janet Rawlins, Angus Rands, Piers Browne, John Cooke, Trevor Burgess and many other talented artists. Paintings are displayed in many village galleries, annual exhibitions of Dales artists' work is held at Askrigg and Grassington, while the Chandler Gallery, Leyburn and the Linton Court Gallery, Settle, have displays throughout the year, the subjects and/or artists being changed monthly.

▲ The clapper bridge at Malham, one of many attractive village bridges

Wharfedale a mile above Kilnsey, one along each side, coming together near Arncliffe and continuing to the valley-head at Halton Gill.

This is Craven country so limestone dominates with scars along green hillsides and bare areas of white rock above Arncliffe, with walls and barns patterning the flat valley floor. Man has found Littondale and its limestone pastures a favoured site since Iron Age times, for the uplands show evidence of early habitations. Anglian settlers utilised well-drained gravel sites for their villages – Arncliffe on the south of the river, Hawkswick, Litton and Halton Gill on the north, nicely spread about two and a half miles apart. In Norman times it was a hunting forest, in medieval days a sheep-rearing estate of Fountains Abbey. After the Dissolution of the Monasteries the pattern of farming changed little – sheep on the hills, cattle in the riverside meadows. Littondale is one of the few valleys in the Dales unscarred by lead mining.

Most of Littondale's magnificent barns, many with covered porches, date from the time when corn was grown here and carts brought under shelter for unloading. Large double doors admitted draught to the stone-flagged threshing-floor. Good examples of such barns can be seen in all Littondale villages, but some have been tastefully converted into private residences, especially at Hawkswick and Litton. These small, linear villages contain good houses and cottages of limestone, with roofs of darker flags, whose shallow pitch echo the slopes of the fells beyond. At the head of the dale Halton Gill is a cluster of mainly 17th-century farms and cottages at the foot of Horse Head pass, an old packhorse route to Raisgill in Langstrothdale.

Riverside paths between Litton, Arncliffe and Hawkswick provide a leisurely way of exploring Littondale, and hill roads out of the valley lead southwards from Arncliffe to Malham or Settle, and from Halton Gill to Stainforth and Ribblesdale. Each traverses the spacious uplands of the Craven limestone; each crosses the line of the Pennine Way, the Halton Gill road passing within a mile of the summit of Pen-y-ghent, the Malham one passing close to Malham Tarn.

MALHAM
MAP REF: 95SD9062

The nearest main road is six miles to the south. From the A65 between Gargrave and Hellifield minor roads lead northwards, converging at Airton and following the youthful River Aire through Kirkby Malham. The sense of high drama increases as Malham is approached and the great limestone cliff of Malham Cove identified beyond the village. Malham is at a focus of the crescent of Craven's limestone country, where the bare bones of landscape come to the surface in cliffs, crags and scars, and man-made miles of limestone walls impose their disciplined pattern on the land. In stage terms Malham is a 'limestone spectacular', a quality known to tourists for two centuries and recognised by the National Park authority by the creation of a large car park (charge) and excellent information centre at the southern entrance to the village. There is virtually no other parking space in Malham, and none along the roads which climb either side of Malham Cove, or on the way to Gordale Scar. To explore the natural beauties of the area visitors are expected to walk, helped by the many miles of waymarked paths and an invaluable local footpath guide. The Malham Landscape Trail (allow about three hours for the four-mile walk) can be followed with the aid of an informative National Park leaflet. This explores and explains the many geological and scenic features of the area.

Malham Beck, which emerges from the foot of the cove, flows down a grassy valley and through the centre of the village, spanned by clapper bridges and a former packhorse bridge, now widened. A sloping green forms the village nucleus, with the Lister Arms above, displaying a handsome date panel, 1723, probably representing a refronting. A stroll around the village reveals many 18th-century datestones on farmhouses and cottages, and there is scarcely a single building which displeases. Trees flourish in this sheltered setting, imparting sylvan overtones to a satisfying harmony of characteristic Dales building. All is stone, mainly limestone, sometimes rendered and whitewashed, sometimes left bare. Mullioned windows are common, and stone roofs universal.

The attractions of the village match the beauty of its surroundings, as a walk along any of the footpaths will reveal. A newly-surfaced stretch of the Pennine Way leads to Malham Cove, ascending by a steep wooden-framed stair the western grassy side of the 250ft cliff, emerging at the top to be confronted by a remarkable limestone pavement with its clints (small flat blocks) and grikes (deep crevices between). The view from the top is sensational and shows, among other things, Celtic fields in the valley. Beyond the top of the cove the dry valley leads northwards towards the water sinks and Malham Tarn.

Gordale Scar, a narrow gorge carved by Ice Age meltwater between frowning limestone cliffs, is one and a half miles east of Malham, perhaps most scenically reached by a field path by Gordale Beck and Janet's Foss, a charming little waterfall. To Malham's west, Pikedaw Hill is another splendid viewpoint, and much less frequented than the cove (see Walk 11). Twin roads north from Malham join near Malham Tarn, then offer the choice of continuing northwards to Arncliffe or westwards to Ribblesdale.

Malham Tarn is a few hundred yards north of the road, and the Pennine Way passes close to its eastern margin. The 153-acre tarn forms part of the Malham Tarn estate, owned by the National Trust. It, together with Tarn House, is let to the Field Studies Council who, throughout the year, run a series of short residential courses, mainly for senior pupils from schools and undergraduates, concentrating on biology and geography. Recently introduced holiday courses for adults wishing to learn more about natural history are proving increasingly popular.

Kirkby Malham has the parish church, characteristically long and low-profiled, wholly 15th century, with stone stocks in the churchyard. Good stone houses grace the village street, and a road to the west crosses the moors to Settle.

MALLERSTANG

MAP REF: 84SD7992 to 78NY7708

When the Yorkshire Dales National Park was designated in 1954 the county boundary between Yorkshire and Westmorland (now Cumbria) formed a convenient northern limit at the watershed between the River Ure, quickly turning eastwards into Wensleydale, and the River Eden, flowing northwards towards Kirkby Stephen. Landscapes do not follow bureaucratic lines, and the upper few miles of Wensleydale and the beginnings of Eden tend to form a continuous trough between the Moorcock Inn on the A684 five miles west of Hawes, and Kirkby Stephen 10 miles to the north. Beyond the county and National Park boundary the valley is called Mallerstang, one of the few north–south valleys in the northern Pennines, threaded by the B6259. It is possible that the National Park will be extended in the future to include Mallerstang.

Austerely beautiful, with scattered farms, a hamlet at Outhgill and a village at Nateby, Mallerstang is flanked by Wild Boar Fell to the west, High Seat on the east, each well over 2,200ft. Becks tumble down from lonely moorland heights; there are few trees. The Settle–Carlisle railway reaches its summit at Ais Gill, 1,169ft, before making the long, winding descent to Kirkby Stephen. On a grassy knoll above the Eden, where Mallerstang begins to broaden and limestone features soften the austerity, are the ruins of Pendragon Castle, repeatedly rebuilt – the last time by their owner, Lady Anne Clifford, in 1660. She also rebuilt, three years later, Mallerstang Chapel at Outhgill, as an inscribed stone above its door testifies. Recently, a fine new set of hassocks has been made by local ladies for the chapel, each illustrating some aspect of Mallerstang, its landscape, history, farming and wildlife.

MASHAM

MAP REF: SE2280

Travellers entering the Yorkshire Dales from the south and east via Ripon and the A6108, cross the river Ure at Masham (pronounced Mass'm) but only skirt the town. Although some distance from the real beginnings of Wensleydale, Masham has for centuries been an important market centre at the eastern edge of the Dales. In the century following the Conquest the de Mowbrays, based on Kirkby Malzeard, owned Mashamshire, but Masham's importance increased during medieval times through the influence of the nearby abbeys of

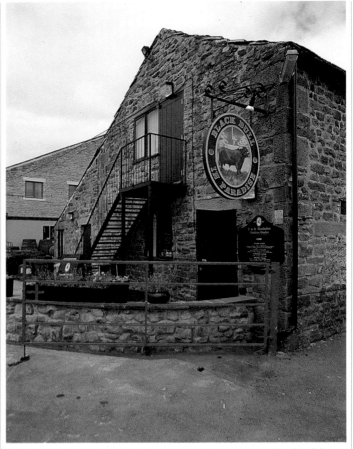

▲ The Theakston Brewery Visitor Centre, Masham, tells the intriguing history of traditional ales since 1821

Fountains and Jervaulx, each of which had many granges and estates in the district. Between 1250 and 1632 the town acquired a series of charters for markets and fairs, most of which were free from tolls, thus gaining trade at the expense of other local markets. By the 18th and 19th centuries Masham's great annual sheep fair in mid-September had grown to be one of the biggest in the north of England, with up to 70,000 sheep and lambs changing hands. They were brought on foot from Swaledale, Wensleydale and Nidderdale, using the old drove roads, most of which are now metalled.

Even into this century Masham's huge, square Market Place would be filled with sheep-pens during the September Fair, and every hotel, house and cottage with spare rooms would be filled. Gypsies camped by the river in what is now a popular open space for summer picnics; there were great family reunions; buyers came from far afield; the church bells were rung.

The great Market Place, partly cobbled, remains Masham's outstanding feature. Surrounded by hotels, inns and houses of grey-brown stone it retains a degree of dignity. A small, tree-shaded market-cross is a

focus, an island group of houses and shops a foil that breaks up the space. At a corner of the square St Mary's church looks south into open countryside. The lower part of its tower is Norman, with an octagonal 15th-century bell-stage added, together with a tall spire – an unusual feature in the Dales area. Outside the south door is the shaft of an important 9th-century Anglo-Saxon cross, showing four tiers of finely-carved figures, human and animal. A Gothick-style school of 1834 by the eastern exit from the square, and terraces of good stone cottages along the road to Kirkby Malzeard complete the impression of an attractive, spacious market town. Masham is also the home of Theakston's brewery, whose most potent brew, 'Old Peculier', commemorates the fact that Masham was a 'peculier' from Roger de Mowbray's time, when the Archbishop of York freed it from 'all customs and claims of his archdeacon and officials.' It was thus allowed to have its own 'Peculier Court' – an ecclesiastical body with wide powers.

The Theakston Brewery Visitor Centre has audio-visual presentations about brewery and cooperage, as well as displays of old tools, pub games and a gift shop – but it is not licensed.

MIDDLEHAM
MAP REF: 87SE1287

Historically – and in the eyes of its 600 inhabitants – Middleham is a township, but with the friendly qualities of a village. Two miles south of Leyburn, on the A6108, it has grown up beneath the protection of its castle whose massive Norman keep dominates the grey stone houses and partially cobbled market squares. If mute stones had voice they would tell of medieval knights and their ladies, the proud Nevilles, the comings and goings of a royal prince, of fairs and festivals, romance and tragedy, trade and commerce, and the generations of townsfolk who had lived their days among the green fields of lower Wensleydale.

The first castle, its site marked by hawthorns, was built in early Norman times. Its successor of 1170 passed into the hands of the Nevilles of Raby a century later, but saw its great days during the Wars of the Roses. In 1461 the young Duke of Gloucester, later Richard III, joined the Middleham household for training and tutorage under the Earl of Warwick, subsequently courting and marrying his daughter Anne in 1472. They made their home at Middleham and their only son, Edward, was born here in 1473. They remained here until 1483, the year that Richard was crowned. He returned north only once more, on the death of his son in 1484. Anne died shortly afterwards and

Richard was slain at Bosworth in 1485. The castle remained Crown property until 1625, eventually passing into private hands, and is now in the guardianship of the Department of the Environment. In 1985 a beautiful, late 15th century Gothic gold pendant was discovered in a field near the castle and a replica of this is now on display.

The Swine Cross in Middleham's upper market place commemorates Richard's 1479 ratification of the market charter given to the town a century earlier by Ralph Neville, Earl of Westmorland. A lane nearby leads to St Alkelda's Church, mainly 13th and 14th century, and made a collegiate foundation by Richard in 1478, continuing thus until the middle of last century, when Charles Kingsley was its last canon.

Three-storey Georgian houses and inns, particularly round the main Market Square, impart an urbane appearance to Middleham. Colourful window surrounds brighten grey stone façades, and varied roof-lines add visual rhythm. Most of the town is a

Middleham's Norman castle was the stronghold of Richard III when he was Protector of the North in the 15th century ▼

conservation area and behind the frontage, narrow alleys hint at former concentrations of cottages.

Near the castle the farrier is kept busy for Middleham is one of the North's great centres for racehorse-training, a tradition going back two centuries. Many Georgian houses in and near the town are trainers' homes, and one set of stables adjoins the castle walls. Over 200 horses are currently trained at Middleham and can be expected at exercise during the mornings on local roads. To the west of the town the 363 acres of Middleham Low Moor provide splendid gallops, the courses marked by lines of whin bushes; High Moor, a few miles to the west, is used more during summer months. Low Moor was the site of one of the great northern cattle fairs, held in late October and lasting three days; cattle were sold on the first day, sheep on the second and odds and ends on the third. It continued to attract large numbers of people until the end of last century but is now only a memory. The road over Middleham Low Moor leads to Coverdale.

▲ This path through stone 'squeezer' stiles and hay-meadows near Muker leads to the River Swale and continues up the valley to Keld

MUKER

MAP REF: 85SD9097

Largest of a trio of delightful villages near the head of Swaledale (the others are Thwaite and Keld), Muker is situated at the southern foot of Kisdon, an isolated hill over 1,600ft high. The valley road from Reeth, the B6270, continues westwards to Thwaite, then by the west side of Kisdon to Keld. The River Swale follows a beautiful valley course to the east of Kisdon and below Muker is joined by Muker Beck.

Grey stone cottages, a popular pub, a church built during Elizabeth's reign, a chapel and an Institute – village additions during lead mining days last century – comprise Muker. Little there may be of architectural pretension but the group in its setting is memorable, with hills, valley and river in noble harmony.

Behind the village are some of the finest traditional hay-meadows in the Dales. In summer they show a rich variety of flowers and grasses, with up

WILD FLOWERS

Vegetation imposes its own broad colour-scheme on the Dales landscape and the type of vegetation is dictated by the soils and rocks beneath. Where there is gritstone, as above Nidderdale, Swaledale and on the higher fells, there are sombre moors, dark for much of the year, purple with heather in August, and often associated with bracken along the edges. But in the limestone country of Craven, Malham and Wharfedale lightness and greenness set the scene, broken by ash woods on the scars. These contrasting colour masses touch on the science of ecology – the relationship of living things to their environment and to one another.

The relatively few plant species of the high fells – for the most part mosses – are dominated by cotton grass, with heather, bilberry and heath. True heather-moors occur between 1,000ft and 1,400ft, sometimes reaching to 1,700ft and down to 700ft on the descending eastern ridges, where tormentil, eyebrights, trefoils and vetches add splashes of colour to grassy swards at the heather's edge. No one species dominates the limestone, and there is more variety, more colour. Where limestone pastures are heavily grazed by sheep, the turf stays short and many small-stemmed plants flourish. In rough ungrazed grassland plants that can compete with the taller grasses may be seen; unmown roadside verges and hay-meadows before cutting provide similar habitats, favoured by knapweed, harebells, early purple orchid, sneezewort and occasionally cowslip. Limestone country is not densely wooded, but the ash which dominates the scars casts only a light shade so that plants which like the damp, lime-rich soils of this woodland floor flourish in such conditions – ramsons, lily-of-the-valley, yellow pimpernel and giant bell-flower. The same ashwoods are also rich in shrub species.

In more acid areas where the parent rock is sandstone or slate foxgloves can be expected on banksides and in open clearings. Sessile oaks are the dominant trees and beneath their heavier leaf canopy fewer ground species grow. Wensleydale, and to some extent Swaledale, with their Yoredale strata of rocks, provide a greater variety of habitat than the other dales, but wherever wild flowers are seen it needs to be remembered that it is now illegal to uproot any wild plant, and even the picking of rare species is prohibited by law. If a flower is picked the seeds from which next season's plants would grow will not be formed. In any case, wild flowers look their best in their natural surroundings.

◄ Foxgloves add summer colour to walls and hedgebanks in valleys, especially on the more acid soils of the northern dales

BIRDS OF THE DALES

The variety of bird life in the Dales reflects the range of landscape habitats. Along most rivers and their tributaries pied and grey wagtails, dippers and common sandpipers nest on shingle banks in the upper reaches and the occasional heron is more likely to be spotted in flight than as a silent, grey sentinel, fish-watching.

▼ Lapwings favour upland pastures

Stone walls are no substitute for the good cover that hedgerows normally provide, although wheatears do like them as perches and song-posts. Deciduous woodlands in gills, on scars, as copses or shelter-belts

offer suitable cover for blackbirds, thrushes, redstarts, chaffinches, willow warblers, spotted and pied fly-catchers, nuthatches, tree-creepers and various tits as well as for the larger birds — rooks, jackdaws, wood pigeons, green and spotted woodpeckers, though these latter are more likely to be heard than seen. One of the smallest birds, the meadow pipit, probably has the widest habitat range, and skylarks are also widespread.

Swifts, swallows and house martins add grace to summer skies, but it is the haunting calls of curlew, lapwing, golden plover and redshank which evoke most vividly the lonelier uplands, the high fells and mosses. Heather moors echo to the harsh rasp of grouse, and it is the elegant black-headed gull which has taken over as breeding grounds, the sky-reflecting tarns of the uplands, coming down to valley fields to feed.

Of birds of prey, kestrels are probably the commonest at lower levels, sparrow hawks less so, while in the remote places buzzards seem to be more numerous than ravens. Most of the predators are holding their own but you need to be sharp to spot merlins, peregrines or short-eared owls.

to a score of different species. To follow the footpath across them (single-file!) and squeeze through a series of narrow stone stiles, is one of the great summertime experiences in the Dales. To continue by the riverside to Keld, returning along the opposite side or by the Pennine Way track high on Kisdon's eastern shoulder, is the best walk in Swaledale. It is small wonder that this district inspired the Kearton brothers (Richard, 1862–1928 and Cherry, 1871–1940), who went to the village school in Muker, to devote their lives to watching wildlife, pioneering the photography of birds and animals, writing and lecturing about their experiences. They are commemorated by plaques on the chapel at Muker.

NIDDERDALE
MAP REF: 93SE0676 to 77SE2459

When the Yorkshire Dales National Park was designated in 1954 its eastern boundary was drawn to exclude Nidderdale, presumably because most of the valley above Pateley Bridge and the surrounding watershed of the Nidd are associated with providing water for

the city of Bradford, and as a result public access to the hills is limited. Nevertheless, the reservoirs — Gouthwaite (1901), Scar House (1936) and Angram (1919) — impart to Nidderdale, even if artificially, a new element to the landscape which differentiates it from the other dales.

Before they entered the scene Nidderdale was the most industrialised of the major Yorkshire dales based on flax-growing and the manufacture of linen and hemp. In addition lead ore was mined and smelted among the hills to the west, but in the upper dale farming predominated, as it still does. The minor road to the upper dale from Pateley Bridge keeps to the

▼ A traditional hay meadow at Muker

western side of the river, passes Foster Beck Mill, now an inn, but retaining its huge over-shot waterwheel, and winds by the side of Gouthwaite Reservoir. This enlargement of a natural lake is a favourite place for wading birds and waterfowl, especially during the winter months, where they like the expanses of mud and marsh at the shallow northern end. Roadside parking is very restricted; a walk from Wath to Bouthwaite along the eastern side of the lake (three miles) is a more rewarding way of seeing the wildlife.

At the head of the lake, Ramsgill is Nidderdale's prettiest village, with grey stone houses informally grouped round two greens separated by a small beck. Daffodils dazzle in late April and trees provide summer shade. Tall, Tudor-style chimneys on the Yorke Arms are unusual accents in a charming village-scape. Two miles beyond, Lofthouse and Middlesmoor are the end villages of the dale, the former's stone cottages and farms huddle at the foot of the steep hill which takes an open moorland road over to Masham in Wensleydale. Middlesmoor's distinction is that it can be reached only by a one-in-four gradient to its hillside perch. Anglican church, Wesleyan chapel, and close-clustered cottages occupy one of the most exposed, windswept village sites in the Dales, 1,000ft above sea-level. The road ends here. However, from Lofthouse a toll road (ticket machine) allows motorists to drive four miles up the valley to Scar House Reservoir, where there are car-parking facilities, picnic areas, and the possible pleasure of a walk round the edge of the reservoir, crossing above it by Angram dam.

Because of the remote situation of these two upland reservoirs a railway was essential to carry building materials during their construction. The Nidd Valley Light Railway was opened in 1907 with a public section between Pateley Bridge and Lofthouse, and a private, waterworks section to the reservoir sites. This had to negotiate gradients of 1 in 40. With Bradford Corporation owning it, the Nidd Valley Line was the only British example of a municipality operating a passenger-carrying railway. After the reservoirs were completed the track was kept open for villagers and tourists, finally closing in 1936, and its course can still be identified.

Near Lofthouse is the spectacular How Stean Gorge, recently developed as a visitor centre. How Stean Beck runs between 70ft rocky cliffs; footpaths, bridges on different levels and fenced galleries on rocky ledges allow the chasm to be explored; Tom Taylor's Cave can also be visited. There is a children's play area nearby.

PATELEY BRIDGE
MAP REF: 97SE1565

Good roads converge on this small town of dour buildings of local gritstone. The B6165 from Harrogate and B6451 from Otley, meeting at Summer Bridge, are joined near Pateley by the B6265 from Ripon, which continues westwards over Greenhow Hill to Grassington. In medieval times monastic estates nearby helped to promote good communications, and Pateley's sheltered situation on the north bank of the Nidd, on the frontier between upland and lowland farming, merited its development as a market centre from the 14th century. Heights of its industrial prosperity were reached about 1800, but when the textile industry became mechanised, its water-powered mills could not compete with steam-powered ones nearer the coalfields. Linen manufacture decreased and Pateley's mills turned to making cord, twine and rope. Stone quarrying and mineral working – mainly lead – survived through last century, but Pateley's present prosperity is based

Set among steep green hills Pateley Bridge is Nidderdale's lively market and tourist town ▼

▲ St Cuthbert's Church at Pateley Bridge replaced the town's only medieval building in 1827

been converted into the Pateley Bridge Dramatic Society's own theatre. Across the river in Bewerley is the early 16th-century chapel which belonged to Fountains Abbey.

REDMIRE
MAP REF: 86SE0491

Five miles west of Leyburn the minor road along the northern side of Wensleydale makes sharp bends through Redmire, whose main axis, unusually, lies north–south. One

outcome of this is that a number of houses down its eastern side are built gable-end to the road, allowing them to face southwards across the valley to the broad, flat-topped bulk of Penhill. Footpaths cross a small, tree-shaded green where the stepped plinth of a vanished cross now supports a Victorian jubilee pillar of 1887, crowned with the recent addition of a lamp.

Narrow lanes bordered by unpretentious cottages of grey stone lead out of the village beyond the green. One of them passes the smithy and the Bolton Arms, leading to Castle Bolton and the moorland road to Grinton in Swaledale. The other passes the King's Arms and the Post Office, which was originally built in 1862 as a drill hall for Volunteers. In the 18th and 19th centuries Redmire was largely an industrial village of craftsmen, lead miners and coal miners who worked at the mines and pits whose remains scar the moors to the north. Today, flower and vegetable gardens give Redmire a degree of colour which makes it less austere than most Wensleydale villages.

Half a mile away to the south-east is the parish church of St Michael, remote and rural, a simple building with a good Norman doorway.

Flower gardens make Redmire one of Wensleydale's most colourful villages. Just south is a small waterfall, Redmire Force ▼

largely on agriculture and tourism. Its fortnightly livestock market survives, and on the Monday nearest to 20 September is Nidderdale Agricultural Society's Annual Show.

Pateley's only medieval building, the old church of St Mary, high above the town, is in roofless decay, abandoned in 1827 when the present church was built in the town. The Panorama Walk nearby commands extensive views of Nidderdale and the moors around, and for those who prefer the riverside there is a convenient free car park at the bottom of the main street. The Nidderdale Museum, recently established, houses a good collection of folk exhibits displayed in nine large rooms, illustrating all aspects of Nidderdale life in the past. Nearby, the Primitive Methodist Chapel has

▲ Pen-y-ghent is one of the famous Three Peaks near Ribble Head where limestone pavements and outcrops are typical of Karst landscapes

REETH
MAP REF: 80SE0399

A dozen miles west of Richmond, by one of the most scenic valley roads in the Dales, Swaledale divides, with Arkengarthdale branching to the north-west and the main valley continuing due west to Muker and Keld. Reeth occupies a commanding position on the lower slopes of Calva, uniting the two valleys but with its feet almost in the Arkle Beck. This gateway situation led to the granting of a market charter in 1695 and in the two centuries which followed it became an important centre of farming and industry, when hand-knitting and lead mining thrived. The village expanded, and seven fairs and a Friday market were held. Now, the population has fallen from 1,300 to 350; Reeth Show in September and the autumn sheep sales are the main annual events, but summer weekends see Reeth Green thronged with people who come just to enjoy the superb setting.

Three-storey houses and inns along High Row testify to Reeth's 18th-century growth which was helped by the turnpiking in 1741 of the Arkengarthdale road from Tan Hill. Houses fringe the sloping green, at whose lower end a former Methodist schoolroom houses the Swaledale Folk Museum, whose range of exhibits illuminate many facets of the local history of Reeth and its neighbourhood. Paintings, pottery and local crafts are exhibited for sale in three local shops or galleries, while beyond the village field and riverside paths are an enticement to walkers.

RIBBLESDALE
MAP REF: 89SD7678 to 94SD8163

Yorkshire's famous Three Peaks, Ingleborough, Whernside and Pen-y-ghent, look loftily if distantly down on Ribble Head, where the road down Ribblesdale, the B6479, branches off the Hawes–Ingleton road, the B6255, near the great railway viaduct. The river is born near Ribble Head House and follows a winding course southwards to Settle, its valley given character by Ingleton to the west and Pen-y-ghent on the east. Low outcropping scars of limestone glisten in sunlight; to the east a huge area of hummocky land extending down the valley almost to Horton with low, rounded hills 50–150ft high, represents the boulder-filled drumlins left by a retreating glacier. It was difficult land to farm so there are no settlements in the upper valley, only scattered farms, this dispersal extending northwards beyond Ribble Head to the feet of Whernside.

Selside is the first hamlet in the dale, where the narrow road twists between two or three farms, and the railway line is close. Other farms nearby underline the fact that this is almost wholly a farming community, and has been since Norse settlers came here a thousand years ago. The railway is only the most recent (1876) of a succession of routes up Ribblesdale – Roman, monastic, medieval, packhorse, drove and turnpike. Many of the old tracks are now green lanes leading to Wharfedale, Wensleydale and Crummackdale.

Horton is Ribblesdale's chief village. Below it the valley narrows, the scars of quarrying gash both the hillsides above Horton and Helwith Bridge – from where narrow lanes lead westwards to Austwick – and the valley's western side to Settle. Slate was quarried at Helwith Bridge and used as cottage floors, doorsteps, porches, gateposts, roofs and headstones, and can be identified in many buildings of Ribblesdale. The main road continues down the east side of the valley touching Stainforth and Langcliffe (see separate entries) before reaching Settle.

The road from Hawes to Ingleton reveals a view of Ingleborough ▼

▲ Richmond's Norman castle has a dramatic terrace walk beneath its curtain wall high above the River Swale, seen here from the bridge

RICHMOND
MAP REF: 81NZ1701

High above the River Swale Richmond's hilltop situation gives it a visual excitement rarely matched in England. Its stones and street-pattern enshrine nine busy centuries of history, imparting a unique character and making it pre-eminent as a gateway to the Dales. Richmond is more than a lively market town; it is an experience. From the A1 at Scotch Corner the A6108 reaches Richmond in four miles, entering the town from the north-east. Only the southern approach, by the A6136 from Catterick, provides the dramatic view of the castle on the rock, and it is the castle (Department of Environment) which commands the scene.

From every angle Richmond's Norman castle dominates the town. At its south-east corner Scolland's Hall, late 11th century, is probably the oldest hall in England. The massive keep, built a century later, and unusual in being at the gatehouse, gives the finest prospect of Richmond from its 100ft high battlements. Far below are the roofs, walls and chimneys, a pattern of pink pantiles, stone slates and Welsh slates. The well-defined limits of the Market Place follow the line of walls of the castle's outer bailey. The medieval town walls were about 50yds beyond them, but only fragments survive, including gateways on Cornforth Hill and in Friar's Wynd.

Narrow streets radiate from the Market Place. New Road, which was new in the 18th century to provide better access to Green Bridge; Finkle Street, one of the medieval streets leading to Newbiggin, new in the 12th century and now Richmond's most elegant thoroughfare, with trees and good Georgian houses; King Street, which dates from 1813, and Frenchgate, the oldest way into the town, but today lined with elegant houses which illustrate the town's commercial and social development during the 18th century. Details in doorways and windows delight the eye,

▲ Narrow streets converge on Richmond's cobbled Market Place

and everything is in small-town scale – except of course, the castle, the splendid view from Castle Walk and the distant Swaledale scenery to the west, along the wooded valley and past Culloden Tower's distinctive shape.

Unusually, St Mary's parish church lay outside the town walls. Holy Trinity, islanded in the Market Place, was never more than a chapel, and now houses the Green Howards Museum. Apart from it and the castle, Richmond's only other medieval building is Grey Friars' Tower, all that remains of a Franciscan Friary. Opposite this is a rare treasure, the Georgian Theatre, dating from 1788 and restored to theatrical use in 1963. Regular productions are presented on its tiny stage before audiences of up to 240 who occupy many of the original seats and boxes in one of the oldest surviving theatre buildings in the country. The Theatre Museum displays a wide range of interesting exhibits including original playbills and painted scenery.

The Richmondshire Museum in Ryder's Wynd is largely a folk museum, and includes among its special displays the famous vets' surgery of the BBC TV James Herriot series.

Although the Market Place provides limited car parking, long-stay visitors are advised to use the large free car park along Victoria Road, 400yds west of the King Street roundabout.

SEDBERGH
MAP REF: 82SD6592

Five miles east of the M6 (Junction 37) Sedbergh is the main western gateway to the Dales and lies just within the National Park boundary. Its position on the A684 Kendal–Northallerton road which cleaves through Garsdale and Wensleydale has further increased its tourist potential as a good base from which to explore the western areas of the Yorkshire Dales, a fact recognised by its good range of accommodation – hotels, guesthouses, holiday cottages, caravan and campsites. Sheltered to the north by the steep-sided Howgills, Sedbergh is the only settlement in the Rawthey valley. The river flows down the eastern side of the hills, partnered by the A683 from Kirkby Stephen, and is joined near the town by the Clough River from Garsdale and Dentdale's River Dee, the combined waters amalgamating with those of the Lune two miles to the south-west.

Above Sedbergh's north-eastern corner Castlehaw was the site of a Norman motte-and-bailey castle. In the town centre, the parish church has Norman origins, and the miniscule Market Place claims charter rights dating from 1251. The main area of weekly stalls (Wednesdays) is in the Joss Lane car park at the eastern end of town. A large livestock market operates from premises in the Kendal road. There is another large car park by the Dent road.

Farms are widely scattered in the valley country around Sedbergh. During the 17th, 18th and early 19th centuries they formed part of the domestic knitting trade which flourished locally. To this was added a cotton industry, based on mills built at Birks, Millthrop, and Howgill. A woollen mill was built at Hebblethwaite Hall and in Sedbergh itself houses were crammed into yards behind the main street. Upper storeys had wooden balconies called spinning galleries, while lower floors were let as stables, stores and workshops. At least one spinning-gallery survives.

In 1525, a famous date for Sedbergh, Roger Lupton, a native of the parish and provost of Eton, founded a chantry school, endowing it with scholarships and fellowships at St John's College, Cambridge. It became a free grammar school in 1552, was rebuilt in 1716 and reconstituted as a public school in 1874, since when it has gained a national reputation. School buildings and playing fields cover most of Sedbergh's southern fringe, but public rights of way through the fields are maintained. The original 1716 building on the Dent road is now a library and museum.

Sedbergh has strong Quaker associations and George Fox preached in the district on many occasions, the most famous one being at Firbank in 1652. Two miles from Sedbergh is Brigflatts, formerly a small industrial community, and its exquisite Friends' Meeting House of 1675, the oldest in the north of England, retains many original furnishings, in an atmosphere of calm, cool tranquility.

▲ The Friends' Meeting House at Brigflatts, near Sedbergh, dates from 1675

SEMER WATER
MAP REF: 85SD9187

A honeypot for summer crowds, a sanctuary for winter wildfowl, Semer Water, situated on the south side of Wensleydale, is the largest natural lake in Yorkshire, half a mile long. Twin roads from Bainbridge lead to the lake, following opposite sides of England's shortest river, the Bain. A link between them touches Semer Water's northern shore, its only access point. Cars can park (charge), and the lake attracts canoers, wind-surfers, yachtsmen and fishermen. Children paddle safely and swimmers brave the cool, shallow waters in summer.

Countersett, on the western road to Semer Water, has strong Quaker associations, with a Friends' Meeting House and some good 17th-century houses, including the Hall (1650) with its two-storeyed porch and stone-mullioned windows. This road ends at Marsett, at the foot of beautiful little Bardale. Above Semer Water's eastern side the road ends at Stalling Busk – merely 'Busk' to locals (it means 'bush') – a hill-clinging community of farms and cottages, with an unusual ruined church in the fields below, and a Roman road climbing the Stake pass above, to Buckden in Wharfedale. The broad, flat valley above the head of Semer Water is Raydale, enclosed by high, lonely fells whose lower sides are now darkened with conifer plantations.

NATIONAL PARK CENTRES

Six National Park Centres have been created to provide visitors with information about the Yorkshire Dales in general, with each Centre having detailed information, especially about its own location. At the centres at Aysgarth Falls, Hawes, Grassington, Malham and Clapham large car parks are available on a fee-paying basis. The car park ticket allows use at all National Park car parks on the day of issue. The Sedbergh centre adjoins a large public car park entered from Joss Lane.

Centres are open daily from Easter to October, each is staffed by an information assistant, and each usually houses an interpretative display relating to its specific area. The Malham centre was purpose built in 1975 and offers an audio-visual display,

particularly useful for visiting school parties. Other centres occupy buildings converted from other use – railway buildings at Aysgarth and Hawes, the old manor-house at Clapham, a cottage at Sedbergh, while at Grassington, it is housed in a purpose-built centre in the main car park.

From various centres throughout the season, with concentrations at Bank Holidays and during July and August, a programme of guided walks is arranged. These start at 2p.m. and usually last 2½–3hrs. Guides are local people with a special interest in some respect of the Dales – local history, flowers, birds, farming, buildings, old industries. The cost is minimal and pre-booking is not necessary. Groups are usually limited to about twenty, and dogs are discouraged! Information about guided walks is given in a free publication, *The Visitor*.

The Yorkshire Dales National Park's emblem is a Swaledale ram ▼

SETTLE
MAP REF: 94SD8163

Like other market towns in the Dales, Settle developed and prospered through its situation between the livestock farming of the uplands and the mixed and arable farming of the lower parts of its valley, in this case the Ribble. Today it benefits – or suffers, depending on your point of view – from being by-passed by the A65 Keighley–Kendal road – busy not only with freight traffic but also with the increasing volume of holiday traffic to and from the Lake District as well as the cars of visitors entering the Dales from the south.

Settle's market charter goes back to 1249, granted for it to serve Ribblesdale and Craven. Market day is Tuesday, when the Market Square is filled with colourful stalls, looked down upon by the unusual, two-storey Shambles, whose arches are probably mid-18th century but whose cottages were raised by a storey late last century. Many stalls and shops support local crafts; expect to find needlework, tapestry, pottery, hand-made jewellery, lampshades and fleeces. Almost all Settle shops are small, independent, with many having been in the same family for generations.

▲ Shoppers at Settle market

Two factors contribute to Settle's 'family atmosphere'. It has remained small, compact and intimate, and it has been faithful to its past, not having destroyed those buildings from the late 17th century onwards which are so important a part of its character. A large free car park on the town's southern edge is not the least of Settle's advantages.

Following the short streets leading from the Market Place – Constitution Hill and Castle Hill, High Street, Victoria Street and Albert Street (which were the old ways into town), Chapel Street, Station Road and Kirkgate – will reveal the yards and squares, cottages, small houses and

THE SETTLE–CARLISLE RAILWAY

Railway historians suggest that the Settle–Carlisle line should never have been built. It arose from a quarrel between two companies, the Midland and the London & North-Western, but built it was, by the Midland, between 1869 and 1876. Constructionally the most difficult, scenically the most dramatic in England, the line follows the Ribble valley above Settle – the famous 'long drag' to Ribble Head, across the heads of Dentdale, Garsdale and Wensleydale, and down Mallerstang to the Vale of Eden and Carlisle. At Garsdale Head it reaches 1,100ft yet the ruling gradient never exceeds 1 in 100. Towering viaducts and bridges, and long, deep tunnels represent a heroic example of Victorian engineering, busy with freight and passenger trains for almost a century.

The 1963 Beeching Report started the decline in its use and local services ceased by 1970 leaving only Settle and Appleby stations open to be served by through trains. However, limited passenger services were revived a few year later through the combined efforts of the Yorkshire Dales National Park Committee, the West Yorkshire Passenger Transport Executive, the Countryside Commission and the county councils of Lancashire

workshops which represent the rapid growth in activity from 1780 onwards, when the development of local crafts, trades and industries reduced Settle's reliance on farming.

By far the most outstanding building is The Folly of 1675, a capricious extravaganza of windows and fine masonry. Tudor in appearance, quite out of Dales character, but undeniably fascinating, it now houses an antiques showroom. A Georgian warehouse overlooks Cheapside, and other Georgian buildings testify to Settle's growing importance when the Keighley–Kendal turnpike brought the coaching traffic to the town, and the resultant need for hotels and inns with which Settle is still blessed. Observant explorers will notice the happy survival of many dated 17th-century door-heads, while the really energetic may accept the challenge of a short steep climb to the wooded top of Castlebergh, a limestone crag above the town, with rewarding panoramic views.

SKIPTON
MAP REF: 96SD9851

With the rich limestone pastures of the Craven uplands to the north, gritstone moors to the south, the broad pastoral lowlands of the Ribble vale a dozen miles to the west, Skipton's situation in the Aire gap ensured its importance as a frontier town, with all the advantages arising from this. Today, major trunk roads meet and cross at Skipton: the A59 Preston–Harrogate road; the A65 Leeds–Kendal road; the A56 from Burnley; the A629 from Keighley. With the B6265 heading north to Grassington, Skipton rightly regards itself as the southern gateway to the Dales, only two miles outside the National Park boundary. A new by-pass has eliminated much through traffic from the town, whose main general market is on Saturday, with stalls in the High Street also operating on Monday, Wednesday and Friday.

A village settled by Anglian sheep-

and Cumbria. 'Dales Rail', as it was called, thrived for over 10 years, serving the needs of walkers from nearby industrial towns as well as local residents. But again the line was threatened with closure and the withdrawal of all services. After years of well organised lobbying and campaigning for its preservation the Settle–Carlisle line was reprieved in 1989 and a regular BR train service now operates throughout the year. 'Sprinter'-type diesel trains, introduced in October 1990, have improved journey times, with six trains running daily in each direction between Leeds and Carlisle throughout the year on weekdays, and a Sunday service of three trains each way from Easter onwards. Additional weekday and Saturday trains run between July and September; all services stop at all intermediate stations along the line. A useful feature is the introduction of regular bus links to serve local towns and villages off the route, including Hawes, Sedbergh, Dent, Brough, Dufton, Keswick and Penrith, as well as Swaledale and upper Wensleydale.

Some of the National Park Committee's guided walks start and finish at stations on the Settle–Carlisle line. (See Walks 9 and 10, pages 110 and 111.)

◀ Settle station marks the start of the 'Long Drag' with the line climbing 600ft in 20 miles

▲ East range, Skipton Castle, 1535

Many High Street properties were rebuilt in the second half of the 17th century and in the 1720s weavers and wool-combers built houses at the bottom end of the town. Thirty years later the Keighley–Kendal turnpike increased Skipton's importance as a wool trading centre, with a livestock market, and by the end of the century the Leeds–Liverpool Canal ensured the concentration of the worsted cloth industry in the town. In 1785 High Mill near the castle was opened as a cotton-spinning mill and early in the 19th century new mills were built by the canal banks. The associated labour needs brought a rapid population growth, long gardens behind High Street properties were in-filled, and many of their yards survive, especially on the west side where tunnel-like openings lead to narrow alleyways with terraced houses along them. Large cotton mills were added to Skipton's townscape between 1850–80, with terrace developments of gritstone houses on the south-eastern slopes above the canal. The town's population doubled from 6,000 in 1871 to 13,000 in 1911, and has stabilised at this figure.

Good parking facilities encourage a long stay and an exploration of the town, appreciating its friendliness, its human scale and lively market-stalls. Two miles east of the town, Embsay Station, opened by the Midland Railway in 1888, now relives its past and houses a railway shop and café. Steam trains run on a 2½ mile trip to Holywell Halt and back, every Sunday throughout the year, more frequently in July and August, with special events on some summer Sundays.

The Leeds–Liverpool Canal adds to Skipton's lively character ▼

farmers in the 7th century it became, in the 12th century, a Norman castle-town under the de Romilles who built their fortress on a rock above the Eller Beck gorge. A market was established at the top of what is now High Street and a three-day annual fair soon followed. Weekly markets concentrated on perishable goods; fairs were more seasonal, dealing with bigger quantities of different commodities – wool, fabrics, metals, leather, salt, wine – bringing traders and merchants from further afield than those involved in the weekly market which was a more local affair. From the 13th to the 18th centuries a town like Skipton with good markets and fairs was virtually self-supporting.

The parish church grew up contiguous with the castle, and the town developed down High Street. In 1309 the castle passed into the hands of the Cliffords, and remained their main home for three and a half centuries. It is still in private hands, open daily, and visitors receive a

40-sketch tour sheet to indicate the most practical viewing route. A very informative descriptive booklet is also available. Entrance is by the proud round-towered gateway surmounted by the Clifford motto, 'Desormais', meaning, roughly, 'henceforth'. After the Civil War, Lady Anne Clifford rebuilt the partially ruined castle, and much of what can be viewed dates from 1655–58 and is splendidly restored.

▲ Stainforth packhorse bridge in a sylvan stretch of Ribblesdale. The bridge, which dates from the 17th century, is owned by the National Trust

northerly of Yorkshire's major dales. Richmond is its eastern gateway, 30 miles from the source of the Swale among the peat haggs and heather 2,000ft up on the lonely uplands of Birkdale Common. A journey westwards up the dale reveals how it is enfolded by unbroken ranges of hills,

STAINFORTH
MAP REF: 94SD8267

Its name derives from the 'stony ford' which linked two settlements half a mile apart on opposite banks of the Ribble north of Settle. Stainforth, on the eastern side, was formerly owned by Sawley Abbey, whose monks developed the estate which prospered, while Little Stainforth, under private ownership, declined. In the 1670s, Samuel Watson replaced the ford by a packhorse bridge (National Trust) whose graceful arch spans an attractively wooded stretch of the river. A grassy path leads downstream to Stainforth Force, where the river falls over limestone ledges into a deep, broad pool. In Little Stainforth the rather forbidding, three-storey Stainforth

Hall was built at the same time and is now occupied as a farmhouse.

Stainforth village is by-passed by the B6479, but a large free car park is an encouragement to stay and saunter among the grey stone cottages centred on a rough green by Cowside Beck, which is spanned by a little clapper bridge. Goat Scar Lane is a stony track leading to Catrigg Force on Stainforth Beck (one mile); Goat Lane is a fine moorland road to Halton Gill in Littondale, with a branch to Malham, while on the west side of Ribblesdale narrow lanes from Little Stainforth lead to Helwith Bridge and Austwick, as well as to Settle.

SWALEDALE
MAP REF: 79NY9000 to 81SE1199

Narrow, sinuous and austerely beautiful, Swaledale is the most

LEAD MINING

Veins of lead ore (galena or lead sulphide) exist in the limestone of the Lower Carboniferous Series, mainly between altitudes of 1,000 and 2,000ft, but because they occur beneath the surface they had to be mined. The Romans worked them, monasteries held mining rights in medieval times, but the main period of activity was during the 18th and 19th centuries, peaking between 1790 and 1860. Most survivals date from then.

Ore fields are concentrated in two areas; in the north Arkengarthdale, Swaledale and the north side of Wensleydale; in the south they extend from Buckden in Wharfedale eastwards to Pateley Bridge in Nidderdale. Early workings were from the surface by shallow bell-pits, later ones by horizontal adits driven into hillsides along the veins of

ore. Suspected veins were revealed (or not) by hushing, a process of scouring a hillside with water released from a temporary small reservoir impounded on the hilltop above. Repeated hushings have left huge gashes on hillsides, especially in Gunnerside Gill and above Langthwaite.

The mined mixture of ore and rock (called bouse) had to be crushed and most of the ore separated by washing. Hence the constant need for water, which was also used to power water-wheels that operated bellows. These helped to force air across the ore-hearth in small furnaces where ore was smelted in order to produce pure lead. Coal or peat was used as fuel but no furnaces or smelt mills survive intact. Their ruins in lonely valleys, and the long courses of flues that dispersed noxious fumes from the mills to distant terminal stacks, remain vivid testimony to a once-

important industry. The most impressive survivals are above Arkengarthdale, above Grinton, at Old Gang, above Castle Bolton, on Grassington Moor, Greenhow Hill and near Pateley Bridge.

Ruins of Old Gang lead-smelting complex ▼

emphasising both its completeness and, towards the valley-head, its remoteness. Such a journey also shows the extent to which man has contributed to the landscape, from the hanging woods in the lower dale between Richmond and Reeth to the soaring stone walls, field barns, farms,

rejoining the Swale at Keld, the last village in the dale. Placenames have their own music, a euphony originating from Norse settlement a thousand years ago. Every village, hamlet, farm and barn is of local grey-brown sandstone from small quarries hidden in the hills. Low-pitched roofs

valley shows its patterned hillsides. At Langthwaite scars and spoil-heaps speak of vanished days of lead mining, and the moorland road to Reeth threads its way between sheep-cropped verges. From the sturdy, black-faced Swaledale sheep comes the warm durable wool which has helped to revive a traditional hand-knitting industry developed over the past few years and boosted by tourism. Small hotels, village pubs, guesthouses, farms and holiday cottages provide a variety of accommodation for visitors who appreciate the serenity of this hautingly lovely valley, its sparkling river and becks, and the lonely, sheep-voiced hills.

THRESHFIELD
MAP REF: 96SD9863

Across the river from Grassington, where the Wharfedale road through Burnsall, the B6160, meets the busier road from Skipton, the B6265, is Threshfield. The heart of the village is the Park, a small triangular remnant of green, with trees and stocks. Seventeenth-century houses and barns cluster round, especially on the eastern side. Date panels signify much activity between 1640 and 1661, with Park Grange and the Manor House, whose tall gable includes a lovely porch with Tudor-style rose window above, prominent. Nearby is a three-doorway barn, or shippon, dated 1661, while opposite is Old Hall Inn, 19th-century at the front, Georgian at the back. Behind it is the original Old Hall, now a store, possibly of 14th-century date. Threshfield Free Grammar School, founded in 1674 by the Reverend Matthew Hewitt, one of the two rectors of Linton, is by the back road from Linton to Grassington that passes half a mile east of Threshfield, and a path leads to it from the village. This delightful little building is still in use as the primary school. Near the hump-backed bridge on the Skipton road a barn door is adorned with horse-shoes and cow-shoes of various sizes, a reminder of the packhorse and droving importance of Threshfield in past centuries.

West of the village a narrow road, metalled for only three miles, leads past the hamlet of Skirethorns and its associated limestone quarry, to Malham Moor. It continues as a green lane to join Mastiles Lane, important from medieval times to droving days last century. The remains of Bordley's prehistoric stone circle are near the end of the metalled road, but to reach the hamlet of Bordley, almost a mile away, footpaths or green lanes must be followed, for there is no road to this loneliest of hamlets on the Craven uplands.

▲ Most farmhouses in the northern dales faced south wherever possible so Birks End, Whitaside, turns its back on a view across Swaledale

villages and remains of lead mining which are so prominent in the upper dale.

The A6108, and then B6270, follow the winding river to Reeth, but the old road along the hills to the north, through Marske and Marrick, though more tortuous in places, is a more exciting way to Reeth. Here the valley divides, Arkengarthdale branching to the north-west and Swaledale aligned due west. A round trip up one and down the other is an excellent way of exploring this wild, northern section of the National Park, whose Pennine character becomes increasingly evident as the dale heads are approached.

Beyond Reeth the B6270 keeps to the northern side of Swaledale, through Healaugh, Feetham and Low Row to Gunnerside, where the road crosses to the south, continuing westwards to Muker. Then it leaves the river for a while to take a course through Thwaite and behind Kisdon,

of stone flags echo distant skylines. Buildings are not beautiful, but their sturdy shapes and textures are in complete harmony with the surroundings.

Hay ripens in riverside meadows, cut in July and stored in a hundred barns. Farming and tourism are Swaledale's main industries now that centuries of lead mining have ended. Field-paths and miners' tracks are invitations to explore Swaledale's intimate delights, particularly in the upper dale.

Above Keld the lonely road to the gathering-grounds of the infant river reveals a different world of bare, sweeping moors, sombre skylines and splendid solitude. It is wilderness country, a similar landscape to that experienced on the West Stonesdale road from Keld to Tan Hill where Britain's highest inn has no neighbour for about four miles. Follow the road eastwards from here and it is five miles before the first enclosed fields appear, and Arkengarthdale's green

THWAITE
MAP REF: 85SD8998

The road up Swaledale, the B6270, takes a northward turn here, where clustered cottages by Thwaite Beck at the foot of Kisdon hill exemplify the characteristic rugged charm of a remote Dales village. A couple of farms, former lead miners' homes that are now holiday cottages, and the well-known Kearton Guest House, comprise this friendly community. The Kearton brothers (see Muker entry) were born here, and a modern, delightfully decorated lintel over a cottage doorway commemorates their birthplace.

Beyond the village the Pennine Way, having descended from Great Shunner Fell, climbs across the face of Kisdon to follow its exciting route above the Swale to Keld. The road takes an equally scenic course through a green landscape, patterned by walls and barns, past Angram to Keld. To the south the Butter Tubs Pass rises to 1,725ft on its wild, moorland crossing to Hawes in Wensleydale. Near the top of the pass, above a steep-sided valley, are the Butter Tubs, a series of limestone swallow-holes near the roadside, deep enough to be dangerous to fall down, yet shallow enough to allow the shade-loving ferns such as hart's-tongue to thrive in them. They can be easily viewed, but their rocky margins are slippery in wet weather and care should be taken. There is roadside parking.

Close-clustered cottages at Thwaite in upper Swaledale ▼

▲ Stone walls and barns, hedgerow trees and scar woods, pastures and hay meadows near Askrigg, Wensleydale with Addlebrough beyond

WENSLEYDALE
MAP REF: 84SD8590 to 87SE1088

Of the major dales Wensleydale is the most pastoral and gentle, green and generously wooded. Even in its upper reaches above Hawes it never achieves the wildness of the lonely, exuberant beginnings of its neighbours to the north and south. During medieval times much of Wensleydale was owned by the Lords of Middleham and Bolton, the Abbots of Jervaulx and and the Metcalfes of Nappa, and it was not until the 16th and early 17th centuries that this large-scale land ownership broke down and the valley became more an area of yeomen-farmers. Good valley pastures and the subsequent improvement and enclosure of land along the hillsides resulted in increased dairying, and today's farming pattern is one in which this predominates, although higher up the dale sheep play an increasingly important part in the rural economy.

Wensleydale is the only dale in the National Park which has, at Bainbridge, a Roman fort. It also has two castles, Middleham and Bolton, two market towns, Leyburn and Hawes, two main feeder valleys, Bishopdale and Coverdale, two important waterfalls, Aysgarth and Hardraw, two National Park Centres, Aysgarth Falls and Hawes, and two roads up the valley.

The main road, the A684, traverses the whole length of the dale as part of an important link between the A1 and the M6, making it particularly popular with visitors. Beyond Wensley it keeps to the southern side and passes through West Witton, Aysgarth and Bainbridge, to Hawes, while the northern road links Redmire, Carperby and Askrigg. Bridges at Aysgarth and Bainbridge provide link roads and the A684 continues as the only westbound route a mile beyond Hawes. On the south side Coverdale and Bishopdale are corridors through the hills to Wharfedale, while from Hawes North Yorkshire's highest road crosses Fleet Moss into Langstrothdale. The B6255 leads southwards to Ribble Head or Dentdale, the Butter Tubs Pass is to the north of Hawes on a minor road leading into upper Swaledale, and moorland roads from Askrigg and Redmire are additional ways over into Wensleydale's northern neighbour.

Wensleydale's villages possess marked individuality – Castle Bolton, Carperby, Askrigg, West Witton and Thornton Rust being markedly linear, Wensley, Redmire, West Burton and Bainbridge delightfully grouped round well-kept greens. Hillsides show a 'stepped' profile, the result of differential weathering of the Yoredale strata, but it is the long limestone scars which are most significant. Penhill and Addlebrough on the south side show familiar plateau summits, the former more easily accessible, and climbable from West Witton Moor. Tracks made by quarrymen, lead miners, packhorses and even Romans encourage easy exploration away from roads, but the more gregarious minded will find their pleasures at Aysgarth, Semer Water and in the market towns of this greenest of dales. Visitors are catered for by a good range of accommodation, and Wensleydale, from just below Leyburn to above Hawes, has more facilities for camping and caravanning than the other dales.

▲ Long horizontal scars etch the hillsides in Wensleydale, and stone barns store the hay used for winter feeding of the stock

WENSLEYDALE CHEESE

The medieval Abbots of Jervaulx were probably responsible for introducing cheese-making to Wensleydale. The formula and method of manufacture have been handed down from one generation to another either by word of mouth or through practical instruction, only relatively recently have written recipes been used. Inevitably local variations have evolved, mainly in Coverdale, Swaledale and Teesdale, but the basic methods have remained the same.

The original cheese was made from ewes' milk, but by the 17th century shorthorn cows were supplanting ewes as milk producers, sheep being bred increasingly for the wool and mutton. Farmhouse cheeses of those days were pickled by salting in brine, and not until 1890 was dry salting introduced. Cheese-making was essentially a summer occupation on farms, largely the responsibility of farmers' wives and other womenfolk, and although some cheeses were for home consumption most went either to the local grocer or corn merchant, usually on the barter system.

At the end of the 19th century Edward Chapman, a Hawes corn and provision merchant, was the biggest local buyer of farmhouse cheeses, and in 1897 he decided to buy milk in bulk from the farms and manufacture the cheese himself. He established the first Wensleydale cheese factory, by Gale Beck in Hawes, based on a daily intake of 200 gallons of milk.

Soon, Alfred Rowntree followed the example and set up factories at Masham, Coverham and Thoralby, using milk from lower Wensleydale, Coverdale and Bishopdale.

In 1945 the newly formed Milk Marketing Board, which had earlier accepted marketing responsibility for the cheese, threatened to close the Hawes creamery, but the late Kit Calvert MBE, of Hawes, opposed this idea. Putting up some capital himself, and persuading local farmers to support him, he bought the factory, where he ran the cheese-making enterprise until his retirement in 1966. During those years a new creamery was opened at Hawes, and in 1963 a larger one at Kirkby Malzeard. Wensleydale cheese is now made at both these creameries. Between them they handle thousands of gallons of milk each day, turning out hundreds of tons

Cheese making at Hawes. Changes have taken place and the maturing process has been speeded up but Wensleydale cheese is still soft, mild and milky and appeals to a wide market ▶

of cheese annually. Although all sizes of cheeses can now be bought in sealed polythene packs the industry still provides cheeses wrapped and matured in the traditional way that has been so successful over the years. Wensleydale cheese can reasonably claim to have 700 years of experience in its manufacture.

▲ High Lane, a Wensleydale track near West Burton

WENSLEY

MAP REF: 87SE0989

A mile south-west of Leyburn this small village of 19th-century estate-style houses round a neat green gives its name to a broad and gracious valley. Scenically, Wensleydale starts here, with the hills along each side becoming more important in the landscape. Above Wensley livestock farming predominates, below are the first arable fields in the dale.

For a century after 1202, when it received its charter, Wensley had the only market in the dale, and this continued to function until the 16th century, though on a decreasing scale as other markets were founded. Plague struck Wensley in 1563 and as the parish register of crops notes, 'This year nothing set down'. Some surviving villagers fled to higher ground at Leyburn, but Wensley revived a century later when Charles Powlett, who had married the daughter of the last Lord Scrope, became Duke of Bolton and built Bolton Hall in 1678, with Wensley the village at its gates. The present Bolton Hall is largely a 1902 rebuilding after a serious fire, but the shell of the 17th-century house survives. There are public footpaths through the Hall's park and woodlands.

Wensley Church is one of the finest in the Dales. Much of it dates from around 1300 but the tower was rebuilt in 1719. The interior is remarkably rich in furnishings, with 17th-century box-pews, a reliquary, a poor-box, a two-decker pulpit, stalls and benches, and communion rail. The Scrope family pew includes part of a fine rood screen which probably came from Easby Abbey at the Dissolution in 1535. There is also a banner of the Loyal Dales Volunteers who were raised against Napoleon, and traces of an early 14th-century wall painting.

West Burton enjoys a superb setting in lower Bishopdale ▶

LIMEKILNS

Like the miles of limestone walls which pattern the Dales landscape the limekilns tend to be taken for granted, yet as many as 700 or more survive from the days when lime-burning was at its peak. By about 1760 a start had been made to enclose land on the moorland edge. After walling, it was burned, drained and limed. Huge quantities of lime were needed; there was abundant limestone, but this had to be burned so kilns were necessary, and it is the cave-like mouths of these which identify their location.

Limekilns are made of dry-stone masonry in the form of squat towers, flat or slightly bow-fronted, 12–20ft across, about the same height, with a funnel-shaped lining of sandstone or brick, cylindrical in its upper part but tapering at the bottom to a narrow neck beneath which is the grate for collecting lime and ash, subsequently raked out from the hearth at the back of the kiln. Limekilns were usually sited at the foot of a limestone outcrop, so that broken lumps of quarried stone could easily be fed into the top, together with alternate layers of coal, ideally obtained from small pits on the moors above. One part of coal to four of limestone would give a good burn, initiated by firing brushwood at the base, and kept charged by adding more limestone and coal, so that its continuous burn could last for two or three days, yielding 300 packhorse loads of 2½cwt each. Four loads constituted a cartful and an acre of land needed ten carts. Many farms had their own kilns. Large kilns or small groups of kilns produced lime on a commercial basis, at four pence a load. Most of the resultant lime was used to sweeten sour moorland soils and make good pasture; some was used in lime-mortar for Dales' buildings, and the use of limekilns lasted for a hundred years from 1760 to 1860.

WEST BURTON
MAP REF: 86SE0186

Off Wensleydale, but not in the main valley, West Burton encapsulates what are all the essential attributes of a village in the Dales. The B6160 Bishopdale to Buckden in Wharfedale road carefully turns away at a corner of the village which is thus conveniently left on no through road to anywhere. Modest houses and cottages of grey-brown stone border a long rectangular green whose focal point is a stepped obelisk of 1820, which is neither a memorial nor a market cross. West Burton never had a market, nor has it a church. Villagers worshipped, were baptised, married and buried, at Aysgarth – hence the number of old field-paths and tracks converging there from villages of lower Bishopdale. Most of West Burton's houses were miners' and quarrymen's properties, and although scarcely a single individual building is outstanding, the whole undoubtedly deserves conservation area status. In setting, shape and appearance West Burton is memorable, with the bonus of a charming waterfall, Burton Force, by the lower end of the village.

Twin roads lead southward into Walden – not a dale by name, but a deeply-cut valley enclosed at its head by the great mass of Buckden Pike, 2,302ft. The western one ends at Kentucky and Walden Head, whence a rough track follows the beck and crosses the watershed into Wharfedale. The eastern valley road is shorter, ending near Low Dovescar. From Whiterow a well-defined grassy track climbs to former coal pits on the moors and drops into Coverdale at Braidley and Horsehouse. Both roads up Walden pass 17th-century farms which are good examples of the characteristic long, narrow buildings of the Pennines.

WHARFEDALE
MAP REF: 91SD9278 to SE1945

Of all the dales' rivers the Wharfe is the most approachable, and from Bolton Abbey upwards to its headwaters of Cam Beck and Oughtershaw Beck over 20 miles away, the road up Wharfedale is never more than a couple of hundred yards from the river. Almost wholly in the Craven Pennines, Wharfedale's scenery is dominated by the Great Scar limestone, and throughout the valley white scars of rock etch the hillsides, sometimes faintly, sometimes with dramatic effect as at Kilnsey Crag.

Anglian pioneers moving up the valley from the east during the 6th and 7th centuries established the pattern of village settlement recognised today – Bolton, Appletreewick, Hebden, Burnsall, Thorpe, Linton, Threshfield, Grassington, Conistone and Kettlewell. Tenth-century Norse settlers from west of the Pennines have given us the farm-hamlets of the upper dale beyond Buckden, itself a village on the edge of a Norman hunting forest. In medieval times Fountains Abbey and Bolton Priory owned great estates in Wharfedale and on the surrounding limestone uplands the pattern of roads and green lanes evolved largely from them, together with the development of market roads and later of drove roads.

Above Burnsall in particular Wharfedale shows the palimpsest of the Enclosure Acts, mainly between 1780 and 1820, when the old common fields were broken up into rectangular pastures enclosed by hundreds of miles of limestone walls in the valley bottom and on the lower slopes of the hills. The memory of the great Cliffords lingers on in the ruins of Barden Tower, and around Bolton. Following the Dissolution, Wharfedale became, eventually, the property of the Dukes of Devonshire, who have, by planting trees, imparted a lush, parkland character to this part of the valley. The Devonshires also revitalised and developed the vast lead-mining enterprises on Yarnbury Moor, above Grassington, but on the whole past industries – corn milling and textiles – have left few discordant remains. Wharfedale is pre-eminently the sylvan dale, best appreciated from the miles of riverside and field paths, always recognisable from a car window.

From below Bolton Abbey two roads lead up the dale as far as Kettlewell, the better one, the B6160, on the western side, but even this is narrow and winding. Every village has its own distinctive appeal, with Linton scoring heavily on account of its grouping round a green with a beck flowing down the centre. Grassington is an important, busy metropolis for the dale, with the charm of a village and the functions of a town – as well as good car-parking facilities. Beyond it, on the eastern side of the dale, Grass Wood is an important nature reserve, and at Kilnsey is a fishing and river-life visitor centre. Nearby is Littondale, with roads to Malham and Ribblesdale, while from Kettlewell a wild upland road crosses to Coverdale.

Wharfedale changes above Buckden, where the B6160 continues over to Bishopdale, but the valley itself narrows, changes its name to Langstrothdale, receives a benediction at Hubberholme church, and its beauty becomes more concentrated as the dale narrows, and road partners a clear river which chuckles over limestone ledges. Woods diminish, except for recent plantations above Beckermonds and Oughtershaw where the winding road climbs over the bleak, bare uplands into Wensleydale.

The upland road from Kettlewell ▼

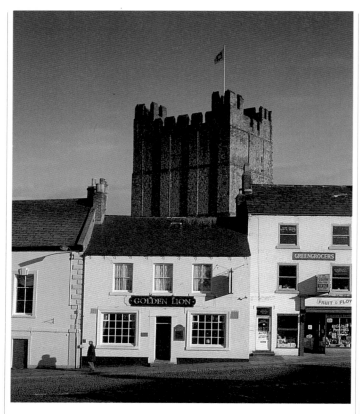

◀ The massive Norman keep of
Richmond castle provides the best
viewpoint of the town

PLACES TO VISIT

Places to visit in the Yorkshire Dales
are listed here under their nearest
town or village and, as a general rule,
correspond to the entries in the
gazetteer section of the book.

The details given are intended to
provide only a rough guide to opening
times. Very often a place may perhaps
be open for part of the day or close
for lunch. Also, although stated as
open all year, many places are closed
over Christmas and New Year. Full
information should be obtained in
advance of a visit from a local tourist
information centre (see page 72).

Many places are owned either by the
National Trust or are in the care of
English Heritage, and if this is the
case the entry is accompanied by the
abbreviation NT or EH.

Telephone numbers are given in
brackets.

BH = Bank holiday
Etr = Easter

AYSGARTH

Yorkshire Carriage Museum, Yore
Mill. *Horse-drawn vehicles housed in
an old stone mill.* Open Etr to Oct,
daily.

CASTLE BOLTON

Bolton Castle. *Stronghold of the
Scropes family where Mary Queen of
Scots was imprisoned for a year.*
Open Mar to Nov, daily; winter,
weekends only.   ▼

CLAPHAM

Ingleborough Show Cave. *Outlet for
Gaping Gill. There is a nature trail
from Clapham to the cave.* Open Mar
to Oct, daily; Nov to Feb, weekends
and by appointment.

FACT FILE
CONTENTS

Places to Visit
Stately homes, gardens, abbeys,
castles, museums and other
attractions

Sports and Activities
Angling, cycling, golf, riding and
trekking, walking

Craft Shops
A selection of workshops
producing original items

Useful Information
Addresses, national park centres,
tourist information centres,
market days, theatres

Customs and Events
A calendar of events

▲

FOUNTAINS ABBEY

Fountains Abbey and Studley Royal (NT). *Huge monastic ruin with landscaped garden and deer park.* Open all year, daily, except Fri in Nov, Dec and Jan.

GRASSINGTON

Upper Wharfedale Museum, The Square. *Dales cottage with farming, lead mining and archaeological exhibits.* Open Etr to Sep, daily.

GREENHOW HILL

Stump Cross Caverns. *Show cave, visitor centre and mineral specimens.* Open Etr to Nov, daily; winter, Sun only.

▲

HAWES

National Park Centre and Dales Countryside Museum, Station Yd. *Agricultural bygones and displays.* Open Apr to Oct, daily; Nov to Mar, some weekends.

INGLETON

(see also **Clapham**). **White Scar Caves.** *Underground formations floodlit.* Open Mar to Nov, daily.

LEYBURN

Constable Burton Hall Gardens, 3½m E of Leyburn. *Large informal garden and a lake.* Open Apr to Aug, daily.

White Scar Caves, near Ingleton ▼

MASHAM

Theakston Brewery Visitor Centre, The Brewery. *The brewing of traditional ales explained.* Open Etr to Oct, Wed to Sun; Nov and Dec, Wed, Sat and Sun.

MIDDLEHAM

Middleham Castle (EH). *12th-century keep dominating the town.* Open Etr to Sep, daily; Oct to Etr, Tue to Sun.

PATELEY BRIDGE

Nidderdale Museum, Council Offices. *Nidderdale life, with Victorian shops and rooms.* Open end May to Sep, daily; Oct to Etr, Sun only; Etr to end May, Sat and Sun.

REETH

Swaledale Folk Museum, Reeth Green. *History, traditions and social history of Swaledale.* Open Etr to Oct, daily; Nov to Etr by appointment.

RICHMOND

Georgian Theatre Royal, Victoria Rd. *Oldest theatre in UK still in original form and still holding live performances.* Open daily, Etr to Oct.

Green Howards Museum, Trinity Church Square, Market Place. *History of the Green Howards Regiment.*

Open Feb, Mon to Fri; Mar, Mon to Sat; Apr to Oct, Mon to Sun; Nov, Mon to Sat.

Richmond Castle (EH). *Ruins with splendid keep.* Open Etr to Sep, daily; Oct to Etr, Tue to Sun.

SETTLE

Museum of North Craven Life, 6/8 Chapel Street. *17th-century building housing exhibitions on all aspects of Craven district life.* Open May to Jun, Sat and Sun; Jul to Sep, Tue to Sun; Oct to Apr, Sat only.

SKIPTON

Bolton Priory, Bolton Abbey. *Ruins of a 12th-century priory set in a park by the River Wharfe.* Open all year, daily.

Craven Museum, Town Hall, High St. *Exhibits relating to the Craven district, including folk life and lead mining.* Open Apr to Sep, Wed to Mon; Oct to Mar, Mon and Wed to Sat. Some BHs.

Skipton Castle. *One of the most complete medieval castles in Britain.* Open all year, daily. See below ▼

STUDLEY ROYAL

SEE FOUNTAINS ABBEY

SPORTS AND ACTIVITIES

The following information is by no means comprehensive and further details can be obtained from the authorities and contacts given. Addresses are listed under Useful Information on page 71.

ANGLING

Most of the Dales rivers and tributaries with game fish are privately owned. Fishing permits can usually be bought locally at village shops and pubs. Rod licences are issued by the appropriate water authorities who also allow game and course fishing on stretches of water under their control; each authority publishes information.

For the rivers Ribble, Lune and Eden, contact the North West Water Authority (rivers division) and for the rivers Aire, Nidd, Swale, Ure and Wharfe, contact the Yorkshire Water Authority (rivers division). In each case see addresses section.

CYCLING

Bicycles can be hired at the following establishments throughout the Dales.

Askrigg, *Ian Rawlins, Woodbin Garage* (0969 663205).

Coverdale, *Thwaite Arms*, Horsehouse (0969 40206).

Grassington, *Cobblestones Cafe*, The Square (0756 752303) and *Pletts Barn Mountain Bikes*, The Mountaineer (0756 752266).

Horton in Ribblesdale, *Three Peaks Mountain Bikes* (07296 200).

Richmond, *Arthur Caygill Cycles* Gallowfields Trading Estate (0748 5469).

Sedbergh, *Sedbergh Cycles*, 61 Main Street (05396 21016).

Settle, Castleberg Sports, Cheapside (07292 3751) and *Settle Cycles*, Station Yard (07292 2216).

Skipton, *Cycle Sport 2000*, 3–5 Water Street (0756 794386) and *Dave Ferguson's Cycles*, 1 Brook Street (0756 795367).

GOLF

The following clubs and courses welcome visitors.

Bentham, *Bentham*, Robin Lane (05242 62455).

Masham, *Masham*, Burnholme, Swinton Road, 1m SW of Masham (0765 89379).

Richmond, *Richmond*, Bend Hagg (0748 3457) and *Catterick Garrison*, Leyburn Road, 1m W of Catterick (0748 833268).

Settle, *Settle*, Buckhaw Brow, Giggleswick, 1m N of Settle (07292 3912).

Skipton, *Skipton*, off North West Bypass, 1m N of Skipton (0756 793922).

RIDING AND TREKKING

Barbon, *River Valley Trekking Centre*, Barbon Fell House, Barbondale (046836 240).

Coverdale, *New Close Farm*, Gammersgill (0969 40668).

Grassington, *Kilnsey Trekking Centre*, Conistone (0756 752861).

Reeth, *Swaledale Trekking Centre* (0748 84581).

Richmond, *Catterick Garrison Army Saddle Club* (0748 832521 ext 2661).

Settle, *Rawlinshaw Trekking Centre*, Austwick (07292 3214).

Semerwater is popular for quiet water-sports and angling ▼

▲ Gouthwaite reservoir provides good opportunities for bird-watching in Nidderdale – and drinking water for Bradford

WALKING

The National Park offers a programme of guided walks in the Dales; full details can be obtained from any of the National Park centres (see this page) or by telephoning 0756 752774.

The National Trust also organises guided walks. These all start from Water Houses, north-west of Malham Tarn and details are available from the warden on 07293 416.

▲ Visitors can see ropes being made at Hawes Ropeworks

CRAFT SHOPS

This is a selection of the craft workshops in the area making original items.

BEDALE

Into Interiors, 29 Market Place. *Farmhouse pine tables and chairs and hand-painted furniture to order.*

GRASSINGTON

Traditional Furniture, Spring Croft, Moor Lane. *Solid oak furniture made by craftsmen.*

HAWES

Hawes Ropemaker, Town Foot. *Skipping ropes to church bell ropes made and sold.*

Jig a Jog Toys, off Market Place. *Traditional toys handmade and painted.*

The Quilt Workshop, Dryden House, Market Place. *Patchwork quilts old and new, plus materials for patchworkers.*

LEYBURN

Sheep Shop, Thorney Grange, Spennithorne. *Wensleydale fleeces, yarns, hand-knitted garments and fabrics.*

LOW BENTHAM

Low Bentham Pottery. *Unusual gifts handmade on the premises.*

MASHAM

Uredale Glass, Market Place. *Free-blown and hand-finished glass and stained glass.*

MUKER

Swaledale Woollens. *Wide range of sweaters and other woollens.*

Gothic style at Settle station ▼

▲ Wensleydale has two market towns. Leyburn's Friday market serves the mid and lower dale

TOURIST INFORMATION CENTRES

Those marked with an asterisk are not open during the winter.

Bentham*, Station Road, (05242 62252/61524).

Horton in Ribblesdale, Pen-y-ghent Cafe (07296 333).

Ingleton*, Community Centre car park (05242 41049).

Kirkby Lonsdale, 24 Main Street (05242 71437).

Kirkby Stephen, 22 Market Street (07683 71199).

Leyburn, Thornborough Hall (0969 23069).

Pateley Bridge*, Southlands car park (0423 711147).

Reeth*, Swaledale Folk Museum, Reeth Green (0748 84373).

Richmond, Friary Gardens, Victoria Road (0748 850252).

Settle*, Town Hall, Cheapside (07292 5192).

Skipton, 8 Victoria Square (0756 792809).

MARKET DAYS

Bentham, Wednesday

Brompton, Wednesday

Hawes, Tuesday

Hellifield, Monday

Ingleton, Friday

Kirkby Lonsdale, Thursday

Kirkby Stephen, Monday

Leyburn, Friday

Masham, Wednesday

Richmond, Thursday (indoor) and Saturday

Sedbergh, Wednesday

Settle, Tuesday

Skipton, Monday, Wednesday, Friday and Saturday

THEATRES

Richmond. *The Royal Georgian Theatre here has hardly changed since the 18th century. Productions range from classical drama to recitals.*

CUSTOMS AND EVENTS

Although the events shown in this section usually take place in the months under which they appear, the dates of many vary from year to year.

Numerous other events such as fêtes and county shows also crop up regularly in the area. Details of what is happening where can be obtained from tourist information centres (see this page) or local newspapers.

The following two events happen more frequently than the remainder,

Swaledale sheep breeders with their ewes at the Tan Hill Show ▼

which are assigned a particular month. Setting the Watch, Market Place, Ripon (held every evening). *The ancient custom of sounding the curfew horn continues today.*

Blowing of the Forest Horn, Bainbridge (held daily from Michaelmas to Shrove Tuesday). *The horn is blown three times each evening for the benefit of people travelling across the moors.*

MAY

Swaledale Festival, Richmond (late May to early June).

JUNE

Grassington Festival, Grassington (mid-June to early July).

AUGUST

St Wilfrid's Feast Procession, Ripon (first Saturday nearest to the first Monday in August). *Celebration of St Wilfrid's return from exile in AD686. Decorated floats follow the procession. Two weeks of sporting events and entertainments follow.*

West Witton Feast and the Burning of Bartle (Saturday nearest 24 August). *An effigy of Bartle is carried around the village and then burned. Bartle's original identity is unknown.*

SEPTEMBER

Beating the Bounds, Richmond (held every seven years, the next one to be held in 1997). *A picturesque procession walks the town's boundaries.*

Atlas

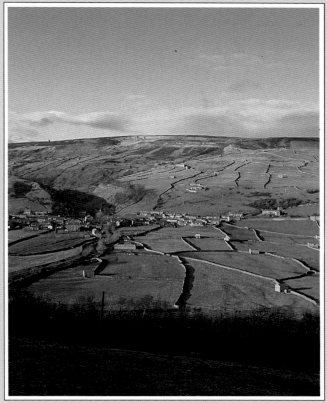

▲ Gunnerside, Swaledale

The following pages contain a legend, key map and atlas of the Yorkshire Dales, two circular motor tours and fifteen planned walks in the Dales countryside.

MAP SYMBOLS

THE GRID SYSTEM

The map references used in this book are based on the Ordnance Survey National Grid, correct to within 1000 metres They comprise two letters and four figures, and are preceded by the atlas page number.

Thus the reference for Hawes appears **84 SD 8789**

84 is the atlas page number

SD identifies the major (100km) grid square concerned (see diag)

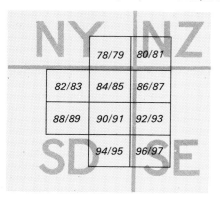

8789 locates the lower left-hand corner of the kilometre grid square in which Hawes appears

87 can be found along the bottom edge of the page, reading W to E

89 can be found along the right hand side of the page, reading S to N

ATLAS 1:63,360–1" TO 1 MILE ROADS, RAILWAYS AND PATHS

M6	Motorway
	Motorway Main road under construction
A 66(T)	Trunk Road
A 685	Main Road ⎫ Single & Dual
B 6270	Secondary Road ⎭ Carriageway
	Narrow Road with passing places
	Road generally more than 4m wide
	Road generally less than 4m wide
	Minor Road, Drive or Track
	Path
	Gradients: 1 in 5 and Steeper 1 in 7 to 1 in 5
	Multiple or Single Track
	Narrow Gauge Track
	Bridges. Footbridge
	Tunnel Cutting
	Freight Line, Siding or Tramway
	Station (a) principal (b) closed to passengers
	Level crossing
	Viaduct Embankment

PUBLIC RIGHTS OF WAY

–·–·–·–·–	Road used as a Public Path
–+–+–+–+–	By-way open to all traffic
··············	Footpath
– – – – –	Bridleway

Public rights of way indicated by these symbols have been derived from Definitive Maps as amended by later enactments or instruments held by Ordnance Survey on 1st October 1984 and are shown subject to the limitations imposed by the scale of mapping.

Later information may be obtained from the appropriate County Council.

The representation in this atlas of any other road track or path is no evidence of the existence of a right of way

Danger Area   MOD Ranges in the area. Danger! Observe warning notices

BOUNDARIES

—+—+— National	—·—·— County
▥ National Park	—+—+— District
NT National Trust	NT always open
	NT opening restricted
FC Forestry Commission	Pedestrians only – observe local signs

GENERAL FEATURES

⌿	Radio or TV mast	P	Post Office
	Church ⎧with tower	PH	Public House
	or ⎨with spire	MP	Mile Post
	Chapel ⎩without tower or spire	MS	Mile Stone
°	Chimney or Tower	LDP	Long Distance Path
	Glasshouse	CH	Club House
	Bus or Coach Station	TH	Town Hall, Guildhall or equivalent
△	Triangulation Pillar	PC	Public Convenience (in rural areas)
⌿	Windmill	VILLA Roman	Castle Non-Roman
⌿	Windpump	⚔	Battlefield (with date)
		✩	Tumulus
		+	Site of Antiquity

╳—╳—╳	Electricity Transmission Line		
>–>–>–>	Pipe Line	♤♤♠	Woods
	Quarry	∷∷∷	Orchard
	Spoil Heap or Refuse Tip		Park or Ornamental Grounds

WATER FEATURES

Marsh or salting

Towpath Lock

Aqueduct Canal Ford

Normal tidal limit

Lake Weir Bridge Footbridge

========= Canal (dry)

HEIGHTS AND ROCK FEATURES

outcrop   cliff   650

600   scree

Contours are at 10 metres vertical interval

·144   Heights are to the nearest metre above mean sea level

Heights shown close to a triangulation pillar refer to the station height at ground level and not necessarily to the summit.

TOURS

2 🚗	Start point of tour	▬▬	Featured tour
→	Direction of tour	⑥	Point of Interest

TOURIST INFORMATION

⚑ ⚑	Camp Site		Nature reserve
⌂ ⌂	Caravan Site	☆	Other tourist feature
🅸 🅸	Information Centre		Preserved railway
🅿 🅿	Parking Facilities		Racecourse
⚝ ⚝	Viewpoint		Wildlife park
⚔ ⚔	Picnic site	🏛	Museum
⚐ ⚐	Golf course or links		Nature or forest trail
	Castle	♍	Ancient monument
	Cave		Places of interest
⚘	Country park	📞	Telephones: public or motoring organisations
	Garden		
⌂	Historic house	PC	Public Convenience
		▲	Youth Hostel
⊕	**Mountain Rescue Post**	with telephone and supervisor
◆ ◆ ◆ ◆	Waymarked Path / Long Distance Path		

TOURS 1:250,000 – ¼" TO 1 MILE ROADS AND RAILWAYS

M6	Motorway with service area and junction with junction number
A 66(T) Dual Carriageway	Trunk road
A 52 Dual Carriageway	Main road
A 685 Dual Carriageway	Roundabout or multiple level junction
B 4407 Dual Carriageway	Secondary road
	Other tarred road
	Other minor road
	Gradient 1 in 7 and steeper

	Road crossing under or over standard gauge track
	Level crossing
	Station
	Narrow gauge track

WATER FEATURES

Cliff
Slopes
Short ferry routes for vehicles
Flat rock
Lake
Bridge Ferry
Transport for vehicles
Low water mark
Canal Dunes High water mark

GENERAL FEATURES

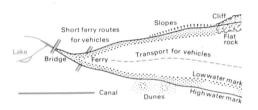

Buildings

Civil aerodrome (with custom facilities)

Wood

Radio or TV mast

Lighthouse

Telephones : public or motoring organisations

ANTIQUITIES

	Native fortress
	Roman road (course of)
Castle •	Other antiquities
CANOVIVM •	Roman antiquity

RELIEF

Feet	Metres	
		.274 Heights in feet above mean sea level
3000	914	
2000	610	
1400	427	
		Contours at 200 ft intervals
1000	305	
600	183	
200	61	
0	0	To convert feet to metres multiply by 0.3048

WALKS

Start point of walk	Line of walk
	Alternative route
Direction of walk	(3) Point of interest

WALKS 1:25,000 – 2½" TO 1 MILE ROADS, RAILWAYS AND PATHS

M1	M1	Motorway	Path
A 64(T)	A 6(T)	Trunk road	Narrow roads
A 515	A 57	Main road	with passing places are
B 6465	B 6105	Secondary road	annotated
A 6(T)	A 57	Dual carriageway	

Road generally more than 4m wide

Road generally less than 4m wide

Multiple track	Level crossing
Single track	Cutting
Narrow Gauge	Embankment
Road over & under	Tunnel
Siding	

Permitted path and bridleway — Paths and bridleways along which landowners have permitted public use but which are not public rights of way The agreement may be withdrawn.

Access Land — Land open to the public by permission of the owner
Access Point

GENERAL FEATURES

Church or Chapel	with tower	Electricity transmission line
	with spire	pylon pole
	without tower or spire	
W, Spr	Well, Spring	Railway station
	Gravel pit	Site of antiquity
	Sand pit	NT National Trust always open
	Chalk pit, clay pit or quarry	NT National Trust opening restricted
	Refuse or slag heap	National Park

HEIGHTS AND ROCK FEATURES

Contours are at 10 metres vertical interval

50	Determined	ground survey
285	by	air survey

Surface heights are to the nearest metre above mean sea level Heights shown close to a triangulation pillar refer to the station height at ground level and not necessarily to the summit

Vertical Face
100
70
50
Loose rock Boulders Outcrop Scree

PUBLIC RIGHTS OF WAY

Public rights of way shown on this Atlas may not be evident on the ground

	Public Paths	Footpath
		Bridleway
+++++	By-way open to all traffic	
	Road used as a public path	

Public rights of way indicated have been derived from Definitive Maps as amended by later enactments or instruments held by Ordnance Survey between 1st April 1984 and 1st July 1984 and are shown subject to the limitations imposed by the scale of mapping.

The representation on this map of any other road, track or path is no evidence of the existence of a right of way.

Key to Atlas pages

Distances in miles to HAWES
Map Ref: 84 SD 8789

Birmingham	164	Leeds	62
Bristol	242	Liverpool	91
Edinburgh	157	Manchester	85
Glasgow	153	Newcastle	75
London	256	Sheffield	110

YORKSHIRE
DALES

0 Kilometres 5 10

0 Miles 5

TOUR 1

DEEPEST DALES AND ROMANTIC CASTLES

Sedbergh, only 5 miles from the M6 motorway, yet overlooked by some of the grandest fell country of the western Dales, is the starting point for this superb tour of the northern Dales, combining mountains, moorland passes and deep valleys rich in heritage and history.

ROUTE DIRECTIONS

The drive starts from Sedbergh①. 83 miles.

Take the main A683 road eastwards from the town, following signs to Brough and Kirkby Stephen.

The A683② switchbacks over open moorland past Kirkby Stephen Common. At the junction with the A685 turn right into the Eden valley to Kirkby Stephen③.

Leave Kirkby Stephen on the B6259 Hawes road as far as Nateby before turning left on to the B6270 signed for Swaledale and Muker. This becomes a steep moorland road climbing the pass between the Eden valley and Swaledale④; care is needed on this road which is narrow in places.

From Reeth keep on the main B6270 to Grinton, but where the main road turns sharp left over the bridge, keep straight ahead up the lane signed for Redmire and Leyburn, keeping to the left fork on the Leyburn road which ascends through open heather moorland past the Catterick Camp Tank Training Area (you must not stop when the red flag is flying) before descending into Wensleydale. Keep ahead at the crossroads into Leyburn⑤. Turn right into the town centre and left into the Market Place.

Follow the A684 out of the town. Turn right after a mile along a lane signed for Harmby and Spennithorne. Beyond Harmby turn right at the junction through Spennithorne, right again at the T-junction down to the Ulshaw Bridge over the River Ure⑥.

Turn right along the A6108 to Middleham⑦. Keep on the main road bearing right towards Leyburn, over the narrow Middleham Bridge over the Ure. Turn left about 500yds beyond the bridge along the lane signed for Aysgarth. At the next road junction, turn right into Wensley village but take the first lane left signed to Redmire and Castle Bolton. Follow this road past Preston under Scar and through Redmire before turning right at the junction signposted to Castle Bolton⑧.

The main route continues along the lane through Carperby, taking the first turn left to go past Aysgarth Falls⑨. Continue up the steep hill to the main A684, turning right and along Wensleydale through Aysgarth village to Bainbridge and on to Hawes⑩.

Continue along the A684 through Appersett and past Garsdale Station on the Settle–Carlisle line before following the winding road through Garsdale to Sedbergh.

POINTS OF INTEREST

① Easily reached from Kendal and the M6 motorway, Sedbergh makes an ideal gateway to the Yorkshire Dales. The town's winding main street, newly recobbled, contains old inns and shops, one of which, at Joss Lane car park, is now the National Park Centre.

② This beautiful road skirts the eastern edge of the Howgill Fells, massive green dome-like mountains which are largely unenclosed common. These fells provide a dramatic backcloth to this section of the route. To the right lie the vast expanses of Uldale and Wild Boar Fell. Cautley Spout, a succession of waterfalls falling 700ft, can be reached by a short walk from the lay-by near the Cross Keys Inn, an 18th-century National Trust hotel, 5 miles from Sedbergh.

③ Kirkby Stephen is an old coaching town lying on a busy cross-Pennine route between Teeside and Lancashire. It has a fine parish church and pleasant riverside walks.

④ There are spectacular views of Upper Swaledale as you descend into this twisting valley, passing a series of lovely stone villages in true Herriot country – Keld, Thwaite, Muker, Gunnerside, Low Row and Reeth.

⑤ Leyburn is a busy Dales market town (market day Friday) with a large central square surrounded by shops.

⑥ Ulshaw Bridge over the Ure dates from the late 17th century; it has the remains of a medieval cross on its parapet.

⑦ Middleham was once a royal town, with a great castle (English Heritage – open to the public), the seat of Richard of Gloucester, later Richard III. A weather-worn statue of his mascot, the wild boar, can be seen in the top square, whilst the many inns indicate the village's former importance as a coaching town.

⑧ Bolton Castle in Castle Bolton village is a magnificent 14th-century castle where Mary Queen of Scots was imprisoned in 1568. It now houses an impressive exhibition of the castle's history, with dungeons and towers, an armourer's forge, banqueting halls and chambers.

⑨ Aysgarth Falls are an impressive series of three waterfalls on the Ure over Yoredale limestone; park in the car park by the National Park Centre. There is also a carriage museum in the old mill.

⑩ Hawes, home of Wensleydale cheese and a busy cattle and local market (market day Tuesday), has a National Park Centre and the Dales Countryside Museum, based on a remarkable collection of Dales agricultural and domestic implements.

TOUR 2

COVE, CRAG AND CAVERNS

The serene priory ruins of Bolton Abbey in its romantic riverside setting and the harsh lines on the horizon left by the lead mining industry are contrasting features of this spectacular drive.

ROUTE DIRECTIONS

The drive starts from Skipton ①. 67 miles.

From the roundabout near the castle follow signs to Harrogate (A59). In ½ mile turn left with the unclassified Embsay road. The former British Rail Station at Embsay is now the headquarters of the Embsay Steam Railway. Near the end of the village turn left, signed Eastby and Barden. Pass through Eastby and ascend on to open moorland from where there are good views. The drive then gradually descends into Wharfedale to reach the junction with the B6160. Here turn right, signed Bolton Abbey ②.

Continue to the Devonshire Arms at Bolton Bridge and turn left on to the A59, signed Harrogate. A climb is then made on to Blubberhouses Moor. The drive enters a rocky valley before the descent into the Washburn valley to Blubberhouses Church, at the head of the Fewston Reservoir. Here, cross the river bridge and turn left on to an unclassified road, signed Pateley Bridge. This road crosses high ground for some 7 miles before reaching the junction with the B6265 where the tour turns left, signed Grassington ③.

Remain on the B6265 and later pass through Hebden before entering Grassington ④.

As the road bears left past Grassington Square entrance, take the next turning sharp right on to an unclassified road, signed Conistone. This pleasant by-road passes through attractive woodland and runs alongside the River Wharfe to the hamlet of Conistone ⑤.

Here keep left, signed Kilnsey and Kettlewell, and cross the river bridge. On reaching the T-junction turn right on to the B6160 and shortly pass beneath the impressive Kilnsey Crag. After another ¾ mile turn left on to an unclassified road, signed Arncliffe. The drive now follows the valley of the River Skirfare to reach the grey stone village of Arncliffe ⑥.

Turn right, signed Litton and Halton Gill, and continue up the valley into Littondale. Pass through the hamlet of Litton and on to Halton Gill, an isolated farming settlement near the head of Littondale. Here turn left, signed Stainforth and Settle, and climb on to open moorland. This narrow, and occasionally gated, by-road reaches a height of over 1,400ft.

After 6 miles turn left, signed Malham. Cross more high ground and in 2¾ miles bear right. Half a mile farther on at the next crossroads turn right, signed Malham, following the narrow lane which descends to Malham village. (It is also possible to visit Malham Tarn ⑦ by going straight over these crossroads and then following the lane back to Malham village ⑧.) Continue through the village to the car park and National Park Centre.

Leaving the car park, turn right towards Kirkby Malham. Here turn left with the main road and follow the valley of the River Aire to Airton. In ¾ mile bear left and cross the river bridge, then pass through attractive countryside. After 2½ miles turn right and continue to Gargrave. Turn left on to the A65, still signed Skipton. In 2¾ miles, at the roundabout, take the second exit for the return to Skipton.

POINTS OF INTEREST

① A busy market town beside the River Aire and the Leeds–Liverpool Canal, Skipton's most notable feature is the castle, dating in part from the 12th century. Other places of interest include the Craven Museum in the Town Hall which covers local history.

② Lying to the left of the road, before reaching Bolton Abbey, is the Strid Woods Nature Trail (the Strid is a narrow and dangerous sandstone chasm carved by the River Wharfe). The surrounding, mainly deciduous, woodlands form a nature reserve noted for its birdlife, wide variety of flowering plants, lichens and fungi. Well-marked trails through the woods allow visitors to enjoy superb woodland and riverside views, as well as abundant natural history. Shortly beyond the Strid stand the ruins of a 12th-century Augustinian priory, on an elevated strip of land overlooking the River Wharfe. Generations of poets, artists and photographers have been attracted to Bolton Priory.

③ Disused lead workings can be seen on the left before passing the entrance to Stump Cross Caverns, once populated by wolverine, bison, fox and reindeer. Some of Britain's finest stalactite and stalagmite formations are shown to wonderful effect by electric coloured lighting.

④ The upper Wharfedale village of Grassington contains a Yorkshire Dales National Park Centre. It is the main tourist spot in the area, with good shops and amenities.

⑤ Conistone's farmhouses, barns and houses are built of local limestone, with rendered walls and dressings of sandstone. The farmhouses and barns are mainly late 17th century.

⑥ Arncliffe is splendidly situated on a well-drained gravel delta above the flood plain of the River Skirfare. The houses, cottages, farms and barns face inwards towards a spacious green.

⑦ The actual tarn – or lake – is a lonely sheet of water set among the moors at an altitude of 1,229ft. It can only be approached on foot.

⑧ The pleasant village of Malham, on the Pennine Way footpath, offers fine walks to three spectacular beauty spots – Malham Cove, Malham Tarn and Gordale Scar. The Cove (to the north of the village) is a limestone amphitheatre with cliffs nearly 300ft high. Gordale Scar (to the north east) is a wild defile containing waterfalls.

THE CORPSE WAY OVER KISDON

The ancient Swaledale Corpse Road over Kisdon Hill forms a high point of this classic walk in Upper Swaledale, rich in geological, botanic and archaeological interest, and offering some of the most dramatic scenery of the northern Dales.

ROUTE DIRECTIONS

Approx. 5½ miles. Allow 3 hours
Start from Muker village car park (grid ref. SE911978).

From the car park walk up into the centre of the village①, past the post office. At the road junction at the top of the village bear right to a path over stiles by buildings, signposted Gunnerside and Keld. Follow the clear path across narrow meadows (walk single file please) and a series of stiles, turning sharp right back to a footbridge over the Swale. Go up the steps and then left along a broad track up above the river.

Cross the stream at a footbridge and follow the higher of two paths. To visit Crackpot Hall②, a fine viewpoint, take the path on the right 400yds after the footbridge to the ruined farm. Otherwise continue ahead through field gates, going sharp left after a bridge over East Gill to reach a path alongside the waterfall and then on to a narrow, enclosed path to Keld③. From Keld walk up to the main road and turn left for 300yds to a gated track④ on the left which ascends Kisdon Hill⑤ (a steep climb).

At the summit keep ahead on the track over the open fell, through gates, and then sharply right into an enclosed way (magnificent views along Upper Swaledale and across Muker). Bear left opposite Kisdon Farm and along the track which descends steeply into the centre of Muker.

POINTS OF INTEREST

① Muker is an exceptionally lovely village in a perfect setting. A former lead mining settlement, it has a traditional pub, a choice of cafes and Swaledale

Woollens, a remarkable shop selling woollen goods made locally using the wool from Swaledale sheep.
② The delightfully named ruined farm of Crackpot Hall takes its name from the cave or pothole of the crows. It is an example of a remote hill farm, now long abandoned, which combined subsistence farming with lead mining. Extensive remains of both lead mining and areas where other ores were worked will be passed on this walk.
③ Originally a Norse settlement (its name means 'spring'), Keld lies on the Pennine Way and is the last hamlet in Swaledale, an isolated community that no longer even has a post office. Close to the hamlet and on the route of this walk are two beautiful waterfalls, Kisdon Force on the River Swale and East Gill Force on a tributary valley.
④ Until the building of Muker Church in 1580, the nearest piece of consecrated ground in Upper Swaledale was Grinton Church (see Walk 2) and when people died in villages or remote farms, their corpses had to be carried in large baskets, supported on the shoulders of carriers, along the traditional 'Corpse Way', which can still be traced as a green bridlepath between Keld and Muker.
⑤ This conical hill forms a unique geological feature in Upper Swaledale, the River Swale having changed course during the Ice Age. The river once ran down the valley to the west of Kisdon Hill, but the creation of a moraine, or dam, from glacial debris in the area of Thwaite caused the river to break through into a tributary valley to the east, rapidly scouring out the present deep, picturesque gorge and turning Kisdon into an isolated green hill.

WALK 2
REETH TO GRINTON

From the former lead-mining capital of
Swaledale, this riverside stroll follows easy
paths between Celtic earthworks to the
'Cathedral of the Dales' at Grinton.

ROUTE DIRECTIONS

Approx. 2½ miles. Allow 1¾ hours
Start from Reeth Green, where you can park on the
cobblestones (grid ref. SE038993)①.

At the south side of the green take the narrow road
between the Congregational church and the Literary
Institute to Back Lane. Turn right along this lane, bearing
left at the fork②.
   At a fingerpost signed Harkside and Grinton, follow
the lane downhill to the left, then the well-trodden path
directly to the Reeth Suspension Bridge. Cross the bridge
and follow the river's edge to the left③.
   After the second stile, the track goes straight ahead
while the river executes an extravagant bow to the left to
be rejoined a little further on. Continue to the minor road,
keeping left to Swale Hall. After about 400yds enter the
churchyard by the gate on the left④.
   Leave the churchyard by the path at its east end and
turn left, noting the 17th-century Blackburn Hall opposite
the Bridge Hotel. Over Grinton Bridge, a footpath on the
left leads across the meadows. The path continues past
Fremington Mill, still retaining its mill race, a discarded
millstone and, out of sight, the crumbling remains of its
waterwheel. Turn left at the road, and cross Reeth Bridge
over Arkle Beck to return to the green.

POINTS OF INTEREST

①Once an important farming and industrial centre, Reeth
is now popular for its superb setting. The Swaledale Folk

Museum, housed in the Methodist Schoolroom, recalls the
local history of the neighbourhood.
②Across the river an ancient earthwork shows as a raised
rampart stretching up the hillside. This and other
earthworks, including Maiden Castle, are all believed to
have been built by the Celtic Brigantes about AD70 as
defences against the Romans.
③From this point, the view back across the river reveals
medieval cultivation terraces and also Reeth Friends'
School. Now a primary school, it was founded by the
Quaker Raw family in 1785. The old spoil heaps from lead-
mining on Fremington Edge are also just visible.
④The Parish Church of St Andrew at Grinton was
founded in the early 12th century. Scratches around the
porch show how retainers sharpened their arrows while
their lords were at service.

Reeth is a fine centre for moorland and valley walks ▼

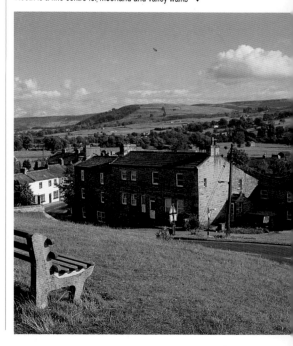

WALK 3

QUAKER QUEST

This delightful but strenuous walk along the shins of the rolling Howgill Fells and the banks of the Lune, renowned for its salmon fishing, visits places of significance in the founding of the Religious Society of Friends.

ROUTE DIRECTIONS

Approx. 5½ miles (plus 2 miles if option taken). Allow 3 to 3½ hours
Park at Sedbergh's Loftus Hill car park (grid ref. SD658920).

Diagonally opposite the car park entrance, take the path beside the churchyard①. Continue along this path past Sedbergh School to its main gates. Across the road, continue up between the houses and the cattle market to the stile, beyond which the path continues up the field to a second stile. Turn right here to the next road crossing. Cross to the farm lane through Lockbank Farm, bearing right to the fell gate. Turn left and follow the steep path along the fellside, with splendid views below. Continue beyond the wood to the sunken-walled lane on the left②.

Go down the lane and turn right along the road to Height of Winder Farm on the left. Take the footpath in front and round the outside of the house garden, through two field gates, and then across the field as indicated by a fingerpost, through stiles, the path descending a field to a hedge and a roadside stile. Cross the road and, keeping the same direction, cross a broken wall, then bear slightly right for a stile beside the electricity pole. The wallside path from here leads to High Branthwaite Farm. Continue past the house and bear left over the footbridge following the path to Draw Well Farm③.

Turn left along the well-defined track past Low Branthwaite to join the River Lune at the disused railway viaduct, then follow riverside field paths to Lincoln's Inn Bridge. Walk with caution along the busy A684 to Ingmire Lodge, then by bridleway to the A683. Turn left, to Brigflatts④, down a lane to the right.

From just above the hamlet an easy footpath leads over the old railway line to Birks. Through this settlement a kissing-gate on the right indicates the path back across the school playing fields to the church and the car park.

A worthwhile extension is to follow the Dales Way right from Draw Well Farm to cross the River Lune below Hole House and ascend directly up Firbank Fell to Fox's Pulpit, the site of the vision's manifestation. Descend to New Field and take field paths to Lincoln's Inn Bridge. Allow an extra hour.

POINTS OF INTEREST

① After the Civil War, a Leicestershire weaver's son, George Fox, dissatisfied with the established church travelled the land to seek a true church. In 1652 on Pendle Hill in Ribblesdale he had a vision of 'a great people in white raiment by a river side, coming to the Lord; and the place that I saw them in was about Wensleydale and Sedbergh'. Soon after, on the day of Sedbergh Hiring Fair, he preached in this churchyard. A local sect called the Seekers shared his beliefs.

② Before going down this lane, 50yds further on, notice the view of the Howgill Fells, some of the wildest hills in the Dales. At their highest they reach over 2,000ft.

③ This private residence, where George Fox stayed after his Sedbergh preaching, was an important early meeting place for the Quaker movement. Just above Draw Well Farm the path meets the Dales Way.

④ The story of Brigflatts is detailed in the Meeting House. One of the first and undoubtedly one of the most attractive, it was built in 1675.

WALK 4
DENTDALE

Dentdale is one of the most distinctive of the Yorkshire Dales, its landscape dominated by two features. The first of these is the great Dent Fault which divides the dale between the typical Carboniferous sandstones and limestones of the Pennines and the more ancient Silurian rocks of the Lake District. The second is a pattern of settlement, Viking in origin, with scattered farmsteads and long, narrow fellside fields — in contrast to the more clustered villages and hamlets of the Anglian settlements in the Dales to the south and east.

ROUTE DIRECTIONS

Approx. 5 miles. Allow 2½ to 3 hours
Start from Dent car park (grid ref. SD704872).

From the car park turn right in the main street ① for 100yds before taking the narrow path right, opposite the end of a chapel, between buildings and over stile. Continue down to the riverside, turning left along the riverbank to rejoin the road after about a quarter of a mile. Keep right, bearing right again back on to the riverside path through stiles down to Barth Bridge. Turn left up the road for 70yds to a stile and footpath along a hedge, going through a gap to the left, between stiles beside the stream to Gawthrop②.

Turn right on the lane through the hamlet, keeping directly ahead at the crossroads and along the narrow lane for 500yds, past Underwood Farm, before soon bearing left up a track past Bower Bank. Keep on the main track, bearing left to Tofts Farm, going through gates at the farmyard and descending to a stream and a small footbridge below. The path now bears left up a slope; head alongside a wall towards a ruined farm, Combe House. Continue around the outside of the house and barn,

along a beautiful raised grassy track below Combe Scar.

Where the track ends, keep ahead in the same direction, beside a wall to reach a ladder stile. Bear right here, around the edge of limestone outcrops, to rejoin the grassy track which leads to a gate and signpost in the corner of a field by the Barbondale road③. Turn right into the road for 500yds and then take a stony track signed Dent to the left④.

Follow this track as it ascends the fell, bearing right then left through gates. At a junction with the Flinter Gill track, turn left through a gate, signed Dent, for a steep descent down a narrow wooded gill into the centre of Dent.

POINTS OF INTEREST

① Once a busy, self-sufficient community and centre of a thriving hand-knitting cottage industry, Dent has declined in importance, though along its narrow, cobbled main street you can still see the tall cottages from whose now-vanished upper storey balconies local people would knit and chat. Dent is also the birthplace of Adam Sedgwick, 1785–1873, one of the greatest geologists of the 19th century (see page 40). The village is well supplied with a choice of cafes and pubs.

② The attractive hillside hamlet of Gawthrop on the lower part of the Barbondale Pass betrays its Viking origin in its name — 'throp' or 'thorpe' meaning hamlet or village.

③ The road between Barbon and Gawthrop follows, very closely, a natural valley formed by the Dent Fault. The change in bedrock will be immediately evident on this part of the walk. The dark, steep, smooth slopes to the right as you approach the pass leading up to Middleton Fell lie on harder, Silurian rock, with a fine example of a glaciated 'cwm' or mountain hollow at Combe Scar. To the left are the limestone outcrops and the gentler moorland summits formed by the Carboniferous rocks of the Pennines.

④ This long track which provides an impressive high-level walk above Dentdale is known as the Occupation Road. It was built in the late 18th century at a time of enclosure to allow farmers or 'occupiers' to reach the high pastures or the open common on the felltops. The beautiful, partially wooded track down to Flinter Gill provides a direct link to the Occupation Road from Dent.

WALK 5

AROUND SEMER WATER

The wide, steep-sided valley of Raydale, off Wensleydale, is a fine setting for the shallow glacial lake of Semer Water, which attracts many human visitors in summer and many avian visitors in winter. Though sometimes marshy in places, this is an easy walk, offering views across the lake as well as visits to the old village of Countersett and to a ruined church.

ROUTE DIRECTIONS

Approx. 3¾ miles. Allow 2½ hours
Start from the north-eastern shore of Semer Water, where parking is available off the road, near the large boulders known as the Carlow and Mermaid Stones (grid ref. SD922876)①.

Cross the bridge over the River Bain (England's shortest river) and climb up the steep hill, turning right at the top into Countersett②.

Return to the crossroads and continue along the metalled Marsett Lane③.

Cross Marsett Bridge and turn left along the track that follows the beck's natural fish nursery. Stalling Busk can be seen at the head of the lane.

Stay on the lane over a footbridge then over another footbridge to a stile by a barn on the left. (A footbridge slightly downstream offers a dry crossing and a short cut!) The path follows a fairly level course through a chain of stiles to a ruined church④.

The path continues to the lake⑤. The road beside Low Blean marks the end of the path, from which an easy few minutes' walk will take you back to the car.

POINTS OF INTEREST

① The Carlow Stone and the two smaller Mermaid Stones near by are huge pieces of limestone left by melting glaciers at the end of the Ice Age. Local folklore attributes them to a fierce stone-throwing fight between the Devil and a local giant who lived on the hill of Addlebrough, a mile or so to the east.

② One of Raydale's three villages, Countersett is a very old settlement with strong Quaker associations. Past the former inn and 17th-century Countersett Hall, a path on the left leads to the Friends' Meeting House.

③ The '-sett' ending of Marsett and Countersett is derived from an Old Norse word meaning 'hill pasture'. It is also found in the names of two nearby Wensleydale hamlets: Appersett and Burtersett. If time permits, a short excursion from Marsett up into the delightful Bardale is soon rewarded.

④ Stalling Busk's little church stood here from 1603 and was rebuilt in 1722. Not until 1909 was this church replaced by one in the village itself, after which the older building fell into ruin.

⑤ The favourite legend about Semer Water runs as follows. An old man, visiting a town that once stood here, asked the inhabitants for food and shelter. All refused, except an aged couple in a poor cottage on the hillside, who took him in for the night. Next morning the beggar pronounced a curse on the town:

'Semerwater rise, Semerwater sink
And swallow all save this li'le house
That gave me meat and drink.'

It rained and rained, flooding the valley and leaving only the cottage where he had stayed. The cries of the drowned, and the town bells, can supposedly still be heard on quiet, dark nights! A tall story, perhaps, but considerable traces of prehistoric settlement were found when the level of the lake was lowered in 1937, leaving scope for conjecture. Today Semer Water attracts windsurfers, swimmers and anglers – and, in winter, large numbers of wildfowl.

WALK 6
BELOW DOVE SCAR

Magnificent views of mid-Wensleydale will be a lasting memory after this walk from the tucked-away village of West Burton, at the foot of Bishopdale. An airy upland track follows a natural hillside terrace before descending to the mysterious ruins of the 'Crusaders' Chapel'.

ROUTE DIRECTIONS

Approx. 4½ miles. Allow 2½ to 3 hours
*Start from West Burton, where you can park beside (not on) the village green (grid ref. SE017867)*①.

At the bottom of the green, take the track to the right, past the old mill, to a packhorse bridge and a spectacular waterfall. Cross the bridge and follow a well-trodden footpath up to a stile, signposted to Barrack Wood. Take the right-hand path at the stile up a steep ascent to the right of Knarlton Knot, then, as it becomes less steep, south-eastwards towards a fingerpost in the wall at the entrance to the disused Hudson Quarry. Follow the quarry road left to join Morpeth Gate above Morpeth Scar②.

The lane, now known as High Lane, winds round the broad terrace below Dove Scar. A walled lane on the left leads down towards Swinithwaite below, with views of Bolton Castle across the valley③.

Where the track, now concreted, swings sharp right, go left across the field between two plantations. In the bottom right-hand corner, a field gate gives access to, and sight of, the ruined chapel across the next field④.

From the chapel cross the lane and follow a level grassy path above Spring Bank Wood⑤.

Beyond a gate in line with the path, descend slightly before emerging on to Morpeth Gate. Follow the lane down to the foot of Barrack Wood. Go through the wood over the stile on the left, then back by the outward route.

POINTS OF INTEREST

①Stone cottages – many of them the former homes of miners and quarry-workers – surround the spacious green at the unspoilt village of West Burton. Peacefully situated off the road through Bishopdale, the village was in existence before the Norman Conquest. The obelisk on the green is of more recent date – 1820 – but it may have replaced an earlier cross.

②The gentle descent down the quarry road affords extensive views up Waldendale, Bishopdale and Wensleydale. The long riggs (ridges) sloping evenly down between the tributary valleys to Wensleydale below illustrate clearly the effects of glacial sculpturing.

③The huge ruin of Bolton Castle dominates much of mid-Wensleydale from its commanding position above the valley at its junction with Bishopdale. The castle was built in 1379 as a fortified manor house, and survived more or less intact until after the Civil War. From July 1568 to January 1569, Mary, Queen of Scots, was imprisoned in the castle, which is now open to the public.

④Described on the map as a preceptory, the name given to a subordinate community of Knights Templars, the ruins here at the foot of Penhill are of a building dating from the early 13th century – some 50 years after the Order of the Knights Templars was established. This chapel was used by the order for a little over a century, until its transfer on dissolution to the Knights Hospitallers. In ruins for over 300 years, it was uncovered in 1840.

⑤Go quietly beside Spring Bank Wood, and you may be rewarded by a glimpse of its resident roe deer.

WALK 7

THE TOP OF WHARFEDALE

Starting and ending at Hubberholme's beautiful and fascinating church, this is a gem of a walk in the most idyllic surroundings. Its easily gained altitude affords spectacular panoramic views of Langstrothdale Chase, a former hunting forest, and of upper Wharfedale's stepped hillsides and small lush meadows. The gentle descent is by the banks of the sparkling Cray Gill.

ROUTE DIRECTIONS

Approx. 3¼ miles. Allow 2 hours
Start from Hubberholme Church; parking may be available in the quiet road over the nearby bridge (grid ref. SD926783)①.

From the field gate next to the church, take the drive which forks right past the church, signposted Scar House②.

The path weaves between the house and a barn, turning sharp right immediately behind the buildings along the edge of limestone rocks behind the sycamore trees on to soft, springy turf. It stays at this level right along the top of Hubberholme Wood③.

Crook Gill is crossed by a footbridge, after which the path turns right and rises slightly to pass in front of a barn, then going past the scattered buildings of a farm to reach the hamlet of Cray④.

The return journey retraces the outward through the farmyard, descending to the left of the last barn and cottage, signposted to Stubbin Bridge to descend to Cray Gill. Following the gill with its numerous cataracts, the path crosses the tributary Crook Gill by an old packhorse bridge⑤.

The gillside path joins the quiet road at Haw Ings. It is only a short distance along to the right to Hubberholme.

POINTS OF INTEREST

① Rebuilt in 1734, Hubberholme Bridge was once on an old and important route between Lancaster and Newcastle. St Michael's Church stands beside it, in a wonderful riverside setting backed by a wooded hillside and distant fells. Indeed the author J B Priestley asked for his ashes to be scattered in the churchyard. The church will unfold its own wonders to the curious visitor, but features to look out for include its rare rood loft dated 1558 (probably removed here about that time from Coverham Abbey), its unusual font – and mice running up and down the ends of the pews! These wooden carvings are the 'signature' of Robert Thompson, who made almost all the 20th-century oak woodwork in the church. Opposite is the George Inn, once owned by the church. Here, the 'poor pasture' is auctioned off each New Year's Day (see page 46).

② The view up Langstrothdale gradually unfolds to reveal bright pastures studded with limestone boulders and rugged outcrops, with hanging woods clinging to the hillsides along the rich limey escarpments. Scar House, with its two date stones, 1698 and 1876, has seen many alterations, but its sturdy construction from local stone, its mullioned windows and its stone slab roof set it clearly in the Dales tradition.

③ Hubberholme Wood consists primarily of species of indigenous trees – ash and wych elm interspersed with hazel, holly and blackthorn, with a sprinkling of oaks and sycamores (although the latter, strictly speaking, are not indigenous). Gradually Buckden Pike appears ahead, and the long glacially widened valley of the Wharfe emerges from the screen of trees, revealing the villages of Buckden and Starbotton melting into their surroundings. After a while a limestone pavement is passed. The grikes (channels) are havens for a variety of flowers – safe from the ever-nibbling sheep.

④ Cray is an old British river name aptly meaning 'clean and fresh'. The hamlet consists of a small farm, a few cottages and the White Lion Inn, a traditional Yorkshire Dales pub offering real ale, morning coffee, lunchtime snacks and evening meals.

⑤ The bed of Crook Gill, often cut deep into the limestone, is studded with potholes and displays many fossils.

WALK 8
CLAPHAM AND CLAPDALE

The nearby geological wonders of Ingleborough Cave and Gaping Gill attract thousands of visitors to Clapham, the starting point of this walk.

ROUTE DIRECTIONS

Approx. 6¾ miles. Allow 3 to 3½ hours
Start from Clapham National Park Centre car park (grid ref. SD745693).

Turn right out of the car park to the top of the village ①. At the church, take the lane (right) that climbs under twin tunnels, signed Austwick. At the corner of Thwaite Plantation turn left into Long Lane, signed Selside ②.

At the end of the walled lane a broad green track heads just below a large cairn on the skyline ahead ③. At a point where the 'lion couchant' shape of Pen-y-ghent just appears ahead, another bridleway joins from the right. Turn along this springy turf track, passing below a band of limestone pavement (not shown on the map), then continue past Crummack Farm for the road to Austwick ④.

As the road sweeps sharply right beyond Sowerthwaite Farm entrance, a stile on the right, signed Norber, leads to Nappa Scars ⑤. Follow the narrow path in front of the cliff-like scars. Continue westwards through a stile on to the open fell ⑥.

From the wall below Norber at the foot of Robin Proctor's Scar, cross the ladder-stile and then walk diagonally across the field, skirting a long-vanished lake to the right to reach a ladder-stile into Thwaite Lane. Turn right back to Clapham.

POINTS OF INTEREST

① The upper part of Clapham village was transformed in the 19th century by local landowners, the Farrer family. They built estate cottages, rebuilt Ingleborough Hall, and dammed Clapham Beck to create a lake, planting thousands of trees on its shores. The Ingleborough Estate Trail was established in memory of Reginald Farrer, the world-famous botanist and plant collector.

② From the beginning of Long Lane the North Craven Fault stretches away to the east below Norber. Massive earth movements long ago created this line of limestone cliffs, which runs right across the National Park. Further up the lane are Thwaite Scars. Glacial erosion and more recent weathering have formed the cliffs and screes here.

③ In Clapham Bottoms, to the left, low rudimentary walls outline ancient field systems, while sink holes indicate the presence of eroded limestone.

④ On the descent towards Austwick, the squat hill of Oxenber stands out to the south-east. Its slopes have the characteristic 'frilled' appearance of terraced hillsides.

⑤ On Nappa Scars, note the breccias, or crushed fragments of rock, between the base of the Great Scar limestone and the much older Ordovician rocks.

⑥ Perched on the limestone shelves of Norber Brow, just above the path, are the huge stones known as the Norber erratics. These dark gritstone boulders were lifted by Ice Age glaciers on their way down Crummack Dale and deposited here.

WALK 9

ALUM POT AND BIRKGILL

This walk takes in characteristic Upper Ribblesdale scenery – high pastures, limestone pavements, green lanes and mysterious pot-holes, with Ingleborough and Pen-y-ghent forming an impressive backcloth.

ROUTE DIRECTIONS

Approx. 8 miles. Allow 4 to 5 hours
Start from Horton in Ribblesdale car park (grid ref. SD807726) or from the railway station.

From Horton①, cross the footbridge behind the car park and walk up the road towards the station, crossing (with care) the level crossing to the kissing-gate and a stile. The path now bears right down a gentle slope, opposite Beecroft Hall farm, to a stile, along a well used way up the hillside beside a wall and over more stiles to level out on a shallow terrace.

Continue straight up a shallow limestone ravine, Sulber Nick②, and as it levels out make for a wooden fingerpost in a concrete base up ahead. Turn sharp right here, signed Selside. The path descends slightly towards a gate; walk 30yds parallel with the wall to a ladder stile at a point where the track bends right. Bear slightly left away from

the wall, heading towards a stile in the wall ahead. Having negotiated the stile, continue in the same direction to reach an enclosed track.

As the track turns right, there is a stile at the intersection of two walls. This stile gives access to a well-used private path which leads across fields to Alum Pot③ (fee payable at Selside Farm). Return to the track and descend to the main road, turning right into Selside. Turn left in the middle of the hamlet by the barn (with a post-box) and the old signal box, signed past Selside Farm. Keep left on the main track down to the riverside, turning right at a gate towards a stile and footbridge. Cross the beck and then bear left to a stile, following the stream to Low Birkwith④.

At the farm, turn left then sharp right on the path between the farmhouse and stream, bearing right to a stile above the slope, and then ahead to stiles through a narrow wood; then turn right on the track leading to High Birkwith Farm. Follow this track uphill towards Old Ing and turn right on to the track (beside a wall) with 'Ribble

Way' signs. Leave the track after Birkwith Cave entrance (in the ravine on the right), bearing right across limestone pavements (care required) down to the ladder stile and footbridge in the shallow ravine below. The path, now clearly marked by ladder stiles along a green terrace, leads past Top Farm. At a ruined barn, turn sharp left to join the Pennine Way near Sell Gill Pot. Turn right to follow this track into Horton.

POINTS OF INTEREST

① Horton in Ribblesdale is the starting point of the popular Three Peaks Walk, parts of which are now suffering from problems of erosion owing to overuse and cannot be recommended. The village has a medieval church and a beautifully kept station on the Settle–Carlisle railway, making it possible to reach the start and finish by train.

② Sulber Nick, a shallow track eroded into the limestone terraces on the shoulders of Ingleborough, may be Iron Age in origin, serving the fortified village on the summit. It now forms part of the Three Peaks Walk.
③ Alum Pot is one of the most terrifying of the great pot-holes of the Yorkshire Dales, descending 200ft to a rocky shelf, below which there is another 100ft drop. The first descent was made by rope, at considerable risk, in 1847. Keep well away from the slippery edge of the ravine. (Access to Alum Pot is across private land and a small payment for the upkeep of footpaths should be made at Selside Farm, in Selside – passed on the walk).
④ Low and High Birkwith are traditional higher Dales sheep farms, both farmhouses and outbuildings probably dating back to the 17th century.

WALK 10

SOUTH FROM SETTLE

Setting out from the old market town that is the southern terminus of the Settle and Carlisle railway, this is a gentle walk in mid-Ribblesdale. Sheltered lanes command views over the dale and into the county of Lancashire.

ROUTE DIRECTIONS

Approx. 3¼ miles. Allow 2 to 2½ hours
Start from Settle's Greenfoot car park, best approached from the A65 at the southern end of Settle, turning into Chapel Street on the right immediately past the police station, then going right along a narrow road, between tall houses, to the signed car park (grid ref. SD821632).

From the car park walk south to the main exit, turning left for 100yds along Ingmire Lane, then take the walled track on the right, Brockhole Lane, signed Mearbeck①.
   At the end of the lane, beside Hoyman Laithe (laithe = barn), cross Lodge Road and follow field paths (in single file) over stiles, to the corner of Cleatop Park②.
   Continue below this wood to enter by the gate half-way along. Follow the diagonal path through the wood to meet another path joining from a footbridge on the right③.
   The route turns sharp left up this path through the pine trees to leave the north-eastern side of the wood by a gated stile. Head across the rough pasture to the field gate just to the right of Lodge Farmhouse. Turn right along the lane for 100yds, then take the walled track on the left which leads to a clear path marked by stiles. This angles down across fields to Brockhole Lane. Turn right and retrace the outward track to the Greenfoot car park④.

POINTS OF INTEREST

① Beyond the allotments on the left as the path leaves Settle are terraced fields – a relic of medieval strip farming. Each strip, called a lynchet, was of a size able to be tilled by a man and his ox-drawn wooden plough in one day. It was believed to be sufficient to sustain a good husbandman and his family throughout the year.
② Pause for a while on the approach to Cleatop Park to take in the view. The south-western horizon is dominated by the heathery Bowland Hills of Lancashire, while to the north the white limestone of Giggleswick Scar and Settle's Castleberg cliff frame the splendour of Pen-y-ghent.
③ Cleatop Park is an old wood now owned by the Yorkshire Dales National Park. Its trees are of many different species and ages, and there is a great variety of woodland plants and birds. In places, clusters of upright, pole-like growth from gnarled stumps reveal the traditional woodland craft of coppicing.
④ Allow time at the end of the walk to explore Settle. This pleasant country town has a long tradition of hospitality towards visitors to the Yorkshire Dales. It owes its Georgian buildings to the prosperity it gained when the Keighley–Kendal turnpike first brought coaching traffic here, and today the town copes admirably with considerable motor traffic on the A65.

WALK 11

PIKEDAW

A walk to enjoy Malham and see many of the famous sights – the cove, the tarn and the remarkable field patterns – without using the busiest and most popular paths.

ROUTE DIRECTIONS

Approx. 3½ miles. Allow 2 hours
Start from the car park (grid ref. SD900627) in Malham①.

Immediately outside the car park turn sharp right along a stony, enclosed track, turning right behind the car park, signed to Pikedaw. Continue for 300yds before taking the second track left which climbs steeply uphill to a fork. Bear left to follow the track down to a stream crossed by a stone-slab bridge.

Make for the stile by the gate to the right and cross a narrow beck towards the barn ahead②. Follow the line of the shallow valley uphill over rough pasture to a ladder stile ahead. Continue in the same direction, recrossing the beck, past a mine adit (1872) to a second ladder stile.

Cross and continue straight ahead to meet the green lane at the summit of Pikedaw③. Bear left to the gate.

Beyond the gate turn right beside the wall, signed Langscar Gate, past Nappa Cross④, bearing right to the gate in the wall below through two more gates. Cross to the corner of the next field and turn right following the sign to Langscar Gate. Pass through another gate and across the third field to join a bridleway. Turn right through a gate and down the track to a stile and cattle grid at the road. Cross the road and go over the stile opposite. Bear right to a ladder stile and then proceed along a grass track through a gap in a collapsed wall, following a well marked path over stiles to Cove Road. Turn right uphill to a bend, going through the gate on the left and along the bridleway, through gates, back to Malham.

POINTS OF INTEREST

① Despite its popular appeal as a tourist centre, Malham village still has some quiet corners, including a number of extremely attractive barns, cottages and farmhouses, several of which are passed on this walk. Note the interesting date stones on several of the buildings and also some fine dovecotes reflecting a time when pigeons were the only source of fresh meat towards the end of a long Dales winter.

② The footpath to Pikedaw runs close to the line of the Mid Craven Fault, a feature of the earth's crust exposing, in this case, underlying limestone rock which has been eroded on the surface to create a dramatic difference in vegetation – pale, green, sweet pastures to the right of the shallow valley through which you climb compared to the rush-filled, dark, acid gritstone moorland to the left – a difference emphasised by the differing colours of the walls.

③ In the late 18th and early 19th centuries Malham was an important area for the production of calamine (zinc ore) which was used, among other things, for the manufacture of brass; vast quantities were taken by pack pony and waggon down to Gargrave from where barges on the Leeds-Liverpool Canal carried it over the new canal network to Cheadle in Staffordshire. A later drain (adit) of the Pikedaw mines is passed on the walk, and remains of the old smelt mill chimney are still to be seen on Malham Moor.

④ Nappa Cross is the base of a medieval monastic cross, formerly placed on the summit of the old road between Settle and Malham. It was restored some years ago and placed in the wall a few yards away from its original position, with a new cross shaft. It is a magnificent viewpoint, looking across to Malham Cove and some of the most impressive limestone scenery in the British Isles, with the shimmering expanse of Malham Tarn and the green pastures of Malham Moor in the background.

WALK 12

YARNBURY AND BARRAS

A walk which explores Grassington's history, from prehistoric settlement to the lead mining which transformed this Dales community into a boom town in the last century.

ROUTE DIRECTIONS

Approx. 5 miles. Allow 2½ hours
Start from Grassington National Park Centre car park (grid ref. SE003637).

From the car park turn left to the village centre①. Walk through the square and up Main Street to the town hall. Turn left along Chapel Street, taking the first steep track right, Intake Lane, just past the Methodist chapel. Follow this uphill to the right through a gate then keep right beside the wall past a barn to a gate and on up to a ladder stile. Keep ahead up the centre of the field to the next stile (where there is a panoramic view) and continue to a further stile which leads into a lane.

Turn left for 400yds and then look for the second narrow stile at the intersection of two walls to the right, signed Hebden Bridleway. Go diagonally across the field to a 'gapstile' in the wall ahead (Woodhenge② is on the

right close to the wall). Keep ahead to a wooden stile by a gate; the path bends slightly left with spoil tips on the left and then leads over stiles ahead, with a pond to the right, before joining a broad track③.

Turn right, but at a fork keep left towards a stile by a gate; then proceed along a track that dips into a shallow valley with a smelt mill and chimney ahead. Before the bridge, look for a gap in the wall to the left. The path goes over heather to a stile into Old Moor Lane (track). Turn left, climbing towards Yarnbury through a gate.

At the junction before Yarnbury House, turn right along Limekiln Lane (enclosed track). Where this track ends at a gate, keep slightly left over rough pasture to another gate ahead and continue through gates beside the wall, bearing left to Barras Farm④. Go through the gate at the far side of the farmhouse, cross the pasture towards a stile ahead and slightly to the right. Descend the long field to a ladder stile in the wall at the bottom right hand corner. Keep ahead across fields by stiles (waymarked), eventually following the wall along the top of the slope which meets a stony track leading to Grassington.

POINTS OF INTEREST

① One of the most popular villages in the Yorkshire Dales, Grassington, with its cobbled square, old lead miners' cottages, excellent local museum, cafes, pubs and shops, lies in the centre of fine walking country.
② Woodhenge is a remarkable prehistoric circle but is easily missed, being little more than a raised grassy circular ridge in the grass. It probably dates from late Bronze Age or early Iron Age times, when the higher limestone terraces were being cleared of scrubland by early farmers, and almost certainly had a religious significance.
③ Grassington Moor is an ancient common, but its minerals, especially lead, have been worked since Roman times. Around Yarnbury it is still possible to see lines of late medieval bell pits as well as the remains of more extensive mining activities of the late 18th and early 19th centuries, when the great Cupola smelt mill (whose tall chimney and flue system creates a major landmark on the moor) was built in Hebden Gill. For those interested in industrial archaeology, there is a National Park trail around the most spectacular remains; please keep to footpaths, as there are many dangerous open shafts.
④ More properly known as Bare House, the remote hill farm of Barras has been unoccupied except as a farm outbuilding for over 40 years. It is private property and in a dangerous state (there is no public access). It is, however, a fine viewpoint. The pastures below the farm, particularly Lea Green and High Close, once contained an Iron Age village; much of this can be seen from the public path.

WALK 13

APPLETREEWICK AND TROLLERS' GILL

A fascinating village and some remarkable limestone formations make this an unusually interesting walk in central Wharfedale.

Approx. 8 miles. Allow 3½ to 4 hours
Start from Burnsall car park (grid ref. SE032612).

From Burnsall car park cross the bridge, at the far side of which is a stile and gate to a riverside path. Keep on this clear path to Woodhouse Farm, through the farmyard and over the stile to the left of the barn to rejoin the riverside path. Continue along the river past the caravan park and then turn left over a stile along the double walled track (Onion Lane) into Appletreewick①.

Walk through the village and turn left past the church and High Hall along Sandygate Lane, but almost immediately go sharp right on a path over a series of stiles up and across narrow fields, descending to New Road. Turn right down to the road junction then turn left through Skryeholme, past the mill and cottages. At a fork in the road bear left. For Parcevall Hall② keep ahead uphill beyond the bridge, otherwise take the gate to the left before the stream marked Gill Head. The public right of way follows the stream up the narrow, rocky valley passing near the entrance to Trollers' Gill③. Take the

path along the left fork over stiles and bearing right to join the miners' track, which climbs up to meet the road from Dibble's Bridge.

Turn left to the road junction, where a gate to the right leads to a stony track across open moor (Appletreewick Pasture). Follow this track over the moor descending to a gate and a stile, keeping ahead and slightly right to reach a gate into Kail Lane (an enclosed track) by Kail Hill④ and Hartlington Hall⑤. At the main road cross over to a farm track to Woodhouse, turning right to retrace your steps to Burnsall.

① Pronounced 'Ap'trick' by locals, this pretty Dales village contains some fine buildings and rich history. This walk utilises Onion Lane where for many years, as part of the popular Appletreewick September Fair, onions were sold in great quantities by itinerant pedlars.

② This walk can be combined with a visit to Parcevall Hall, a carefully restored 17th-century house, now an Anglican retreat, whose superb terraced gardens are open to the public during the summer months.

③ This complex of narrow, rocky valleys and caves forms a remarkable geological feature linked, in Dales folklore, with the occasional appearance (in moonlight) of a giant ghostly dog known as 'The Barguest'. It was also a centre for lead mining and water from many gushing underground springs was used for reservoirs to power local mills.

④ A fine example of a limestone reef knoll, Kail Hill was formed rather in the fashion of a coral reef in primeval seas during Carboniferous times. Reef knolls are a remarkable feature of this part of Wharfedale.

⑤ Hartlington Hall, rebuilt in 1894, was the seat of an important medieval Wharfedale family, the Hartlingtons. There is a picturesque old mill with a waterwheel close by which was powered by the waters of Barben Beck.

WALK 14
STRID WOODS

One of the most romantically beautiful woodland and riverside walks in England through a rocky gorge intertwined with footpaths carefully constructed to take advantage of the spectacular views, and focusing on the awesome Strid, a narrow cataract through which the whole of the force of the River Wharfe plunges.

ROUTE DIRECTIONS

Approx. 4½ miles. Allow 2 hours
Start from Cavendish Pavilion car park (grid ref. SE077552)①.

From the entrance to Strid Woods② follow the former carriage drive for a mile to the Strid③. A narrow path (care required) climbs away from the edge of the river along rocky crags before descending back to the riverside. Keep ahead to a footbridge and stile at the edge of the wood.

Continue on the river bank past the Nidderdale Aqueduct (over which the walk can be shortened) to Barden Bridge. Turn left uphill to Barden Tower④.

From Barden Tower return to Barden Bridge, this time crossing the bridge and going through the gate at the far side to the path on the far bank. Continue along the riverside, past the aqueduct, the path climbing to re-enter the wood at a stile. Continue on the top path, again with magnificent views across the Strid, finally descending to the riverside. The path eventually climbs up to the lane at a bridge over Posforth Gill. Cross the bridge, taking the path to the right which leads back down to the riverside, emerging at the wooden bridge over the river to Cavendish Pavilion.

POINTS OF INTEREST

①Cavendish Pavilion, a popular cafeteria, shop and meeting place, lies close to the entrance to Strid Woods, with overflow riverside car parking. The car park charge covers admission to the Woods, which are owned and managed by the Chatsworth Estate, most of the paths not being public rights of way. (An electric carriage is available to take people unable to walk the one mile between the pavilion and the Strid. This can be booked in advance from Bolton Abbey Estate Office, telephone 0756 71227).

②A wide variety of soft and hardwood trees, including beech, oak, ash, holly, larch and willow, gives these magnificent, mature woods colour and interest at any season of the year and provides habitats for many birds, small mammals, ferns, mosses, fungi and lichens. Many of the footpaths and viewpoints were laid out by The Reverend Carr, scholar and vicar of Bolton Abbey early in the last century, with carefully planned seats and viewpoints, many of which are now being restored. The Strid Woods Nature Trails offer a choice of routes for the more adventurous, in addition to the one described here.

③The Strid is a deep – and dangerous – natural chasm in the sandstone riverbed of the Wharfe, scoured out by the continual flow of water. The name 'Strid' comes from 'stride' and many people over the centuries have drowned trying to leap the narrowest point (which under no circumstances should be attempted). One famous casualty occurred in Norman times when the Boy of Egremond, heir to the great Romilly estates, was, according to legend, dragged to his death by his greyhound. Despite (or even because of) such tales, this remains a hauntingly beautiful and awe-inspiring place.

④During the Wars of the Roses this medieval hunting lodge was the home of Henry, Lord Clifford, the 'Shepherd Lord', son of the notorious 'Butcher' Clifford. Afraid for his safety, his mother sent him to Cumberland to be brought up as a shepherd's son and when at the age of 32 he inherited his estates after the Battle of Bosworth in 1485 he returned to the Dales a simple shepherd. He was then taught by the monks of nearby Bolton Priory, soon becoming a notable scholar and statesman. The Shepherd Lord enlarged Barden Tower around 1500 and continued to live there; it was restored by Lady Anne Clifford in the 17th century and is once again being repaired to preserve it for posterity.

WALK 15
SHARP HAW

Sharp Haw is one of the most spectacular hills in the southern Dales. Though a mere 1,171ft high, it commands impressive views of the Craven Hills and the Aire Gap. It is an easy climb from the market town of Skipton, whilst the return route via the hamlet of Flasby and the towpath of the Leeds–Liverpool Canal is filled with historic and wildlife interest.

ROUTE DIRECTIONS

Approx. 8½ miles. Allow 3½ to 4 hours
Start from Skipton Town Hall car park (grid ref. SD992518).

From the High Street go past the church and Springs Branch Canal bridge to the Gargrave road, taking the next turn right into Chapel Hill. Where the road forks, bear left up to a step stile by a gate. Keep ahead to the next stile① on the brow of the hill ahead, then dip down to the A65; cross with care. Keep ahead across the golf course, with the path first following the left of a wall and then the right of a hedge down to Brackenley Lane. Turn left to the Grassington road; cross the road to a stile ahead and follow the path over several stiles to a lane. Turn right and follow the lane round three bends; at the third bend take a gate on the left leading to a track.

Where the track bends left bear slightly right at a fingerpost along a path marked by posts. This leads over the moor to a gate in the fence ahead. Now head for the summit② of Sharp Haw (there is a permissive path to the summit). The bridlepath bears right across heather to a gate in the wall ahead, then right to a second gate towards Rough Haw. Follow the clear path to the left through the bracken. This winds down the hillside and becomes a farm track into Flasby③.

In Flasby turn left along the track in front of a wall with a post-box, over a stile to the right before going through a gate and then left along a waymarked path in front of Flasby Hall. Cross the park to a stile on the Grassington road. Turn left for 500yds, then left again over a stile at a road junction opposite the turning to Malham. Head for a point left of the wood on the hillock ahead. Go over a stile in the fence and keep ahead, descending through a gate and stiles to the edge of a wood to join the Leeds–Liverpool Canal by an aqueduct④.

Cross the canal at the footbridge by the locks and continue along the towpath⑤ (three miles level walking) into Skipton. (The walk can also be shortened by turning right into Gargrave for bus and rail services into Skipton.)

The Leeds–Liverpool Canal at Gargrave, near Skipton ▼

POINTS OF INTEREST

① The fields crossed on the first section of the walk once formed part of the enclosed medieval park of Skipton Castle. It was from Park Hill, at a point close by the second stile on the walk, that Cromwell's soldiers had a gun battery during the Civil War and from where, in a three-year long siege between 1642 and 1645, Skipton Castle was fired upon. Cannon-balls are still occasionally discovered in the former moat, now the Spring Branch of the Leeds–Liverpool Canal. Skipton Castle was the last Royalist stronghold in Yorkshire to surrender to Parliamentary forces.

② This craggy gritstone summit with its less spectacular twin, Rough Haw, form a notable landmark and viewpoint, offering an impressive panorama of the gritstone moors and fells to the north including, to the north-east, Crookrise Crag and the heather-covered expanse of Barden Moor. To the south-west lies Lancashire's Pendle Hill, but perhaps the most impressive feature of all is the great Aire Gap. This is one of the most significant natural gaps in the central Pennines through which the River Aire,

Leeds–Liverpool Canal, former turnpike road and Leeds–Carlisle railway wind their way to link the busy West Yorkshire towns with the North-West and Scotland.
③ This delightful hamlet remains a typical small Dales farming community away from traffic and tourist trails. Flasby Hall, though partially demolished and undergoing restoration, is an early Victorian country mansion in Italiante style. Its fine parkland is a feature of this walk. Please keep to the waymarked path through the grounds.
④ This 127-mile long trans-Pennine waterway reached Gargrave from Leeds in 1777 but was only finally opened all the way to the Atlantic port of Liverpool in 1816, owing to the economic effects of the Napoleonic Wars. It was a broad (14ft) canal and was designed by John Longbottom of Halifax on the contour principal to take advantage of natural features in order to minimise the number of locks and the necessity for water supplies. For a time Gargrave was its northern terminus, and its wharves became an important transhipment point for lead from the Grassington Moor mines and zinc ore from Malham Moor (see Walks 11 and 12) which was taken by barge to Leeds, Hull and the Midlands. The canal's existence did much to stimulate the industrialisation of the towns of the Aire valley, including Skipton, which still has many former canalside warehouses and mills, many now being adapted to new purposes. Many of these old mills are passed on this walk.
⑤ The winding towpath of the Leeds–Liverpool Canal between Holme House and Skipton passes between a number of smooth-shaped grassy hillocks known as 'drumlins'. These consist of huge mounds of clay, boulder and gravel deposited here by the retreating Airedale glacier as it carved its way through the Aire Gap during the last Ice Age. They have blended into the landscape to form a distinctive feature and their shape has been likened to a basket of eggs.

ACKNOWLEDGEMENTS

The Automobile Association wishes to thank the following photographers, libraries
and associations for their assistance in the preparation of this book.

E A Bowness 8 The Strid, Wharfedale; *J Fell* 22 Mountain Marathon, 23 Potholers; *L Fellows* 16 Dalesman
Clark Stones; *J Forder* 14 Leck Fell, 23 Potholer; *M Hartley & J Ingliby* 10 Bolton Castle, 11 Howgill Hay
Stone, 25 Trotting Race; *M Kirby* 24 Underground Stone Mine; *Mary Evans Picture Library* 46 George Fox;
World Pictures Cover Towards Upper Winskill; *G Wright* 6/7 Swaledale, 9 Roman Rd, Bainbridge, 11 Haytime
Littondale, 26/7 Pennine Way, 28 Above Malham Cove; *M Wright* 13 Malham Cove

All remaining pictures are held in the Association's own library (AA Photo Library) with contributions from:
M Adelman, A Baker, P Baker, J Beazley, E A Bowness, R Czaja, R Eames, S & O Mathews,
C Molyneux, J Morrison, M Trelawny, W Voysey.

Other Ordnance Survey Maps of the Yorkshire Dales

How to get there with Routemaster and Routeplanner Maps

Reach the Yorkshire Dales from Manchester, Leeds or Carlisle and other parts of Northern England
with Routemaster sheet 5.
Alternatively use the Great Britain Routeplanner which covers the whole country on one map sheet.

Exploring with Landranger, Tourist and Outdoor Leisure Maps

Landranger Series
1¼ inches to one mile or 1:50,000 scale.
These maps cover the whole of Britain and are
good for local motoring and walking. Each
contains tourist information such as parking,
picnic places, viewpoints and rights of way.
Sheets covering the Yorkshire Dales are:
  91 Appleby-in-Westmorland and surrounding area
  92 Barnard Castle and surrounding area
  98 Wensleydale & Upper Wharfedale
  99 Northallerton, Ripon and surrounding area
103 Blackburn, Burnley and surrounding area
104 Leeds, Bradford & Harrogate area

Outdoor Leisure Series
2½ inches to 1 mile or 1:25,000 scale.
These maps for walkers show the countryside in
great detail, including field boundaries and rights of
way in England and Wales.
Yorkshire Dales – Western Area
Yorkshire Dales – Southern Area
Yorkshire Dales – North and Central Area
Teesdale

Touring Map and Guide Series
1 inch to 1 mile or 1:63,360 scale
No. 6 Yorkshire Dales

Other titles available in this series are:
Brecon Beacons; Channel Islands; Cornwall; Cotswolds; Days Out from London; Devon and Exmoor;
East Anglia; Forest of Dean and Wye Valley; Ireland; Isle of Wight; Lake District; New Forest; Northumbria;
North York Moors; Peak District; Scottish Highlands; Snowdonia; South Downs; Wessex.